THE southern kitchen garden

THE southern

kitchen garden

vegetables, fruits, herbs, and flowers
essential for the southern cook

WILLIAM D. ADAMS
and THOMAS R. LEROY

Taylor Trade Publishing
Lanham • New York • Boulder • Toronto • Plymouth,UK

Published by Taylor Trade Publishing
An imprint of The Rowman & Littlefield Publishing Group, Inc.
4501 Forbes Boulevard, Suite 200, Lanham, Maryland 20706

Distributed by NATIONAL BOOK NETWORK

Library of Congress Cataloging-in-Publication Data
Adams, William D.
  The southern kitchen garden : vegetables, fruits, herbs, and flowers essential for the southern
  cook / William D. Adams and Thomas R. LeRoy.
    p. cm.
  ISBN-13: 978-1-58979-318-7 (pbk. : alk. paper)
  ISBN-10: 1-58979-318-8 (pbk. : alk. paper)
  1. Vegetable gardening—Southern States. 2. Fruit-culture—Southern States. 3. Herb
gardening—Southern States. 4. Flower gardening—Southern States. 5. Kitchen gardens—
Southern States. I. LeRoy, Thomas R. II. Title.

SB321.5.S74A33 2007
635.0975—dc22
                                    2007009989

♾™ The paper used in this publication meets the minimum requirements of American National Standard for Information Sciences—Permanence of Paper for Printed Library Materials, ANSI/NISO Z39.48-1992.

Manufactured in the United States of America.

contents

acknowledgments and dedication

This book is dedicated to the four great kitchen gardeners who most influenced my life and passion for gardening. First, there were my grandfather and grandmother—John and Bertha Mount. Their entire backyard was a garden. Except for the perennial beds where poppies, peonies, and iris flourished, Grandfather dug the garden by hand every spring. They planted, cultivated, and harvested the garden of approximately 35 × 150 feet; then my grandmother would can the vegetables that would help to sustain them through the winter. I remember the shelves of jars with neat curtains that lined the back wall in their small bathroom. I remember creamed green beans and crisp fried okra—country food—to fuel hardworking farmers. I didn't know my grandparents when they lived on a farm, but Grandfather still helped his son with the wheat harvest, and I eventually worked for him, too—driving a wheat truck, plowing, and hauling hay.

In the summer before the seventh grade, we moved to the same town where they lived, shortly after Grandfather passed away. Not knowing anyone in the town and having long ago discovered the fascination of gardening, I spent most of the summer with my grandmother looking at seed catalogs and searching the garden daily for choice morsels. Grandmother died that fall, and I moved on to school, new friends, and kid stuff, but Mom and I always planted a small garden or at least a few tomato plants. When it came time to go to college, I decided to study horticulture. I wasn't sure how to make a living at my chosen profession, but I was sure I had a passion to learn about it.

I met George and Mary Stewart several years after taking the position of county extension horticulturist with Texas A&M University in Houston, Texas. We became great friends and I visited their garden often to take pictures and check on the progress of the test plants they were trying, and, as was their custom, I always left with fresh vegetables after enjoying one of Mary's fabulous home-cooked meals. George and Mary didn't just walk the walk; they could talk it, too. They became regulars at our garden schools presenting their educational and very entertaining programs. George loved to tell a joke, and Mary was there to play the "straight man" or later on to help with the punch line if George stumbled a bit.

They both gardened into their 90s and lectured until the last few years. They were really more "family" than friends, and I miss their wit and wisdom very much.

I think this is book project number nine, so I've dedicated books to just about everybody, but I would be remiss not to thank my mother Marge; my wife Debbi; my wonderful children Holly, Teneil, and Corinn; and the six grandchildren—Trenton, Ashley, Landen, Turner, Koy, and Conner—for their love and support. I also owe a debt of gratitude to my friends Clyde and Carolyn Cannon, Grady and Virginia Joiner, and Brian and Lorraine Koehl for helping us in the construction phase of our kitchen garden. My mother-in-law Mabel has been babysitter and chief irrigator to the garden, and my sister-in-law Cindy has also been a big help. Even our dog, Simba, has done his part by walking us three times a day to ensure that we stay fit enough to work in the garden.

Finally, I owe Nancy McClanahan, Montgomery County Master Gardener, a sincere thank you for her wonderful illustrations of the garden planting plans that I roughed out. "Roughed out" really doesn't suffice for a description—they were so rough, we thought some of my scribblings to represent plants were actually text. Thanks, Nancy!

—William D. Adams

During the past 30 years of my professional career there have been so many professional horticulturists and master gardeners that have contributed to my overall knowledge and experience of gardening. Gardening is one of those adventures that is difficult to learn but, rather, must be experienced. I want to express my sincere and heartfelt thanks to all of those great gardeners and horticulture professionals who have helped by sharing their experiences with me. My wife pointed out to me the other day that I really didn't have a job these past 30 years. I have been blessed with a career that allows me to go to work every day to do something that I truly love to do and will continue to do long after I've stopped getting paid for it.

I would like to acknowledge my two daughters, Christie and Niki, and my five incredible grandchildren who have the ability to add so much joy to my life. Tyler Lane, Jordan Moore, Lauren Moore, Kyle Whitehead, and Blake Whitehead show me every day, through their amazement of the world around them, the value of gardening and teaching others about the wonders of planting a seed and watching it grow. One of the most amazing ways to garden is through the eyes of a child.

I would like to dedicate this book to my best friend, my wife Sandy. The one thing I can always count on in this world is her support and love. She is my greatest fan, providing me with the confidence to know that anything can be done if you want it badly enough. There is no way that I will ever be able to thank her enough for all those little things she does every day to make my life a little brighter.

—Thomas R. LeRoy

acknowledgments and dedication

introduction: history of the kitchen garden

A kitchen garden is a constant reminder to celebrate the changing seasons—it is close by, brimming with vegetables, herbs, flowers, and even fruit trees. It's our link with nature and a source for fresh produce ready for the table in its time. The French call it a *potager*—usually constructed in formal fashion but with an informal mix of vegetables, herbs, and flowers. Typically berries were encouraged around the fringes of the potager; even a dwarf peach or plum wasn't out of place. It's a theme that has persisted for centuries in Europe, and with our current compact and carefully planned landscapes, it's a concept that has merit for anyone wanting more than azaleas and meatball-shaped evergreens.

The kitchen garden was a lot more commonplace in the rural South than most of our current urban generation might imagine. It wasn't referred to as a potager or even a kitchen garden—it was just "the garden." At times it meant the difference between being well fed and going to bed hungry. Our parents' generation was a lot closer to the farm, and they often remark that "even during the Depression folks on the farm weren't hungry." They make this statement mostly because these families had big kitchen gardens, orchards, hogs, cows, and chickens. The store shelves might have been a little bare, and the gas to drive into town may have been scarce; but if you had enough strength after a hard day's work, you could harvest from the garden and maybe throw a chicken in the pot to prepare a hearty supper.

getting started

Your personal potager can be as simple as a 4 × 6 foot box made with scrap 2 × 8s or as elaborate as a series of geometric beds constructed with a rock border. Although it is not absolutely necessary to raise the beds, even sixteenth-century artwork showed garden beds raised above the surrounding soil level. In most areas of the South, good drainage is often lacking, so the raised bed concept just makes sense.

Location and soil preparation are the keys to success when it comes to any gardening effort. Most vegetables, herbs, flowers, and fruits will do best growing in full sun—6 to 8 hours minimum. There are exceptions—leafy vegetables and root crops will tolerate more shade, mints grow well in the shade, many flowers will thrive in shade, but not many fruit crops will produce in the shade. Citrus species are a possible exception as they often do well in partial shade.

Soil preparation is the area where most gardens either fail or thrive. The more good organic matter you can find, the better. Organic matter comes in many forms, and most of it is good, but the way you use the various forms is critical. Compost is the ideal product—it can be mixed with the soil and will add nutrients and a living population of beneficial organisms. If you have enough, you could even use it as mulch. This is wasteful use of "black gold" for most of us, though. We use our valuable compost as a soil amendment, and less decomposed products like bark mulch or grass clippings go into the garden as mulch on top of the soil. Here they serve to retain moisture, reduce soil heat, and keep down the weeds. If these high-carbon products were mixed with the soil, the micro-organisms would tear into them as a food source and in the process tie up nitrogen and other nutrients that our garden plants need to grow. Since the micro-organisms have a higher affinity for these nutrients, our plants will be yellow and stunted. Chances are you couldn't add enough fertilizer to the soil at one time to compensate for this tie-up without burning the plants. If you do get into a situation like this, it is best to foliar feed once or twice a week to keep your garden plants growing actively without burning them.

Late spring kitchen garden with onions, kale, brussels, sprouts and edible podded peas.

What about using chemical fertilizers? Obviously most foliar fertilizers are soluble chemical fertilizers, though I suppose you could use a watering can or a pump-up sprayer with fish emulsion or liquid seaweed to supply foliar nutrients. The ionic form in which nutrients enter the plants' root cells is the same regardless of the origin—chemical or organic. So, it makes sense for most gardeners to judiciously use some chemical fertilizer to ensure good growth and production. Where most beginning gardeners get into trouble is dumping a handful of 12-24-12 into the planting hole with a tender tomato plant only to watch it wither and die. Fertilizers are salts, so they have to be used according to directions, or you'll be singing the "Harsh Chemical Fertilizer" blues with the rest of the gardeners who got a little too generous with the fertilizer.

You can also be firmly under the "organic banner" without feeling deficient or needing to apologize for your philosophy—actually most folks brag about their organic posture. Organic techniques aren't necessarily easier because you don't spray or use harsh fertilizers. In reality, you will spray more often with less toxic materials, and you will haul heavier, lower-nutrient-content organic fertilizers into the garden. This isn't all bad. Exercise is good, and organic fertilizers contain a lot

Organic Gardening

My good buddy, the late George Stewart, used to claim, "I'm an organic gardener until I see the first bug." In George's defense, he meant that he used tons of organic matter in the garden and held off spraying as long as he could, but he wasn't about to do all that work and not have gorgeous vegetables to give to his friends.

Vegetables	Two Months before Last Freeze	One Month before Last Freeze	LAST FREEZE DATE	One Month after Last Freeze	Two Months after Last Freeze	Three Months after Last Freeze
Beans (Bush)			■■■■■■■■■■■■■■■■			
Beans (Pole)			■■■■■■■■■■■■■■■■			
Beans (Lima)			■■■■■■■■■			
Beets	■■■■■■■■■■■■■■					
Broccoli		• • • • • • • •				
Brussels Sprouts	• • • • •					
Cabbage	■■■■■■	• • • • •				
Cabbage (Chinese)		■■■■■■■■■				
Carrots	■■■■■■■■■■■■■■■					
Cucumbers				■■■■■■■■■■■■		
Eggplants				■■■■■■■■■■■■■■		
Endive	■■■■■■■■■■■■■■■					
Kale		■■■■■■■■■■				
Kohlrabi		■■■■■■■■				
Lettuce (Leaf)		■■■■■■■■	• • • • •			
Lettuce (Head)		■■■■■■■■				
Melons (Honeydew)				■■■■■■■■■■■■■■		
Muskmelons				■■■■■■■■■■■■■■		
Mustard Green		■■■■■■■■■■■				
Okra				■■■■■■■■■■■■■■		
Onions (Plants)	• • • • •					
Parsley	• • • • • • • • • • • • • • • •					
Parsnips		■■■■■■				
Peas (English)		■■■■■■■				
Peas (Edible Podded)	■■■■■■■■■■■					
Peas (Southern)				■■■■■■■■■■■■■■		
Peppers				■■■■■■■■■■■■■■		
Potatoes			■■■■■			
Pumpkins				■■■■■■■■■■■■■■		
Radishes		■■■■■■■■■■■■				
Spinach		■■■■■■ • • •				
Squash (Summer)			■■■■■■■■■■■■■■			
Squash (Winter)			■■■■■■■■■■■■■■			
Sweet Corn			■■■■■■■■■■			
Sweet Potatoes (Snips)				• • • • • • • •		
Swiss Chard		■■■■■■■■■■■				
Tomatoes			• • • • • • • •			
Turnips		■■■■■■■■■■■				
Watermelons				■■■■■■■■■■■■■■		

• • • • = *Transplants only*

Vegetables	Four Months before First Freeze	Three Months before First Freeze	Two Months before First Freeze	One Month before First Freeze	LAST FREEZE DATE	One Month after First Freeze
Beans (Bush)		▬▬▬				
Beans (Pole)		▬▬				
Beans (Lima)		▬▬				
Beets		▬▬▬▬				
Broccoli			▬▬ • • • •			
Brussels Sprouts			▬▬ • • •			
Cabbage			▬▬ • • • • • • • • • • •			
Cabbage (Chinese)		▬▬▬				
Carrots			▬▬▬▬▬▬			
Cauliflower			• • • • • • •			
Celery			• • • • • • •			
Chicory			• • • • •			
Cucumbers	▬▬					
Eggplants	▬					
Endive		▬▬▬▬				
Garlic		▬▬▬▬▬				
Kale			▬▬ • • • • •			
Kohlrabi			▬▬ • • • • •			
Leeks			▬▬			
Lettuce (Leaf)			▬▬▬			
Lettuce (Head)			▬▬▬			
Melons (Honeydew)	▬					
Muskmelons	▬					
Mustard Green		▬▬▬▬▬▬				
Okra	▬					
Onions			▬▬			
Parsley		▬▬▬▬▬▬▬				
Parsnips			▬▬▬▬▬			
Peas (English)	▬▬▬					
Peas (Edible Podded)	▬▬▬					
Peas (Southern)	▬					
Peppers	• • • •					
Potatoes		• • • •				
Pumpkins	▬					
Radishes		▬▬▬▬▬▬▬				
Rhubarb		• • • • • • • •				
Spinach			▬▬▬▬			
Squash (Summer)	▬▬					
Squash (Winter)	▬▬					
Sweet Corn	▬▬					
Swiss Chard		▬▬▬▬▬▬				
Tomatoes	• • • •					
Turnips		▬▬▬▬▬▬				
Watermelons	▬					

• • • • = *Transplants only*

the southern kitchen garden

STATE City	Spring (Date) Freeze Probability (Percentage)			Fall (Date) Freeze Probability (Percentage)		
	90	50	10	10	50	90
ALABAMA						
Anniston	Mar. 15	Mar. 30	Apr. 13	Oct. 21	Nov. 1	Nov. 12
Birmingham	Mar. 13	Mar. 29	Apr. 14	Oct. 24	Nov. 6	Nov. 18
Dothan	Feb. 21	Mar. 13	Apr. 1	Oct. 31	Nov. 15	Nov. 30
Florence	Mar. 13	Mar. 27	Apr. 10	Oct. 22	Nov. 4	Nov. 17
Gadsden	Mar. 20	Apr. 4	Apr. 18	Oct. 18	Nov. 2	Nov. 17
Huntsville	Mar. 26	Apr. 9	Apr. 22	Oct. 9	Oct. 25	Nov. 10
Mobile	Feb. 6	Feb. 27	Mar. 19	Nov. 5	Nov. 26	Dec. 17
Montgomery	Feb. 22	Mar. 11	Mar. 28	Oct. 29	Nov. 12	Nov. 25
Tuscaloosa	Mar. 5	Mar. 22	Apr. 8	Oct. 20	Nov. 4	Nov. 20
ARKANSAS						
El Dorado	Mar. 14	Mar. 28	Apr. 11	Oct. 24	Nov. 5	Nov. 18
Fayetteville	Apr. 8	Apr. 21	May 3	Oct. 4	Oct. 17	Oct. 30
Fort Smith	Mar. 22	Apr. 3	Apr. 14	Oct. 18	Oct. 30	Nov. 12
Helena	Mar. 9	Mar. 25	Apr. 10	Oct. 20	Nov. 6	Nov. 23
Hot Springs	Mar. 7	Mar. 23	Apr. 8	Oct. 27	Nov. 9	Nov. 21
Jonesboro	Mar. 15	Mar. 29	Apr. 11	Oct. 23	Nov. 5	Nov. 19
Little Rock	Mar. 13	Mar. 28	Apr. 13	Oct. 15	Oct. 31	Nov. 15
Pine Bluff	Mar. 2	Mar. 19	Apr. 4	Oct. 26	Nov. 8	Nov. 22
Texarkana	Feb. 23	Mar. 12	Mar. 29	Oct. 29	Nov. 14	Nov. 30
FLORIDA						
Daytona Beach	Jan. 9	Feb. 8	Mar. 11	Dec. 1	Jan. 4	Feb. 9
Fort Myers	—	—	Feb. 10	Dec. 26	—	—
Gainesville	Feb. 5	Mar. 3	Mar. 29	Nov. 5	Nov. 27	Dec. 18
Jacksonville Beach	Jan. 17	Feb. 14	Mar. 14	Nov. 16	Dec. 14	Jan. 13
Lake City	Feb. 21	Mar. 10	Mar. 27	Nov. 5	Nov. 22	Dec. 8
Miami	—	—	—	—	—	—
Orlando	—	Jan. 28	Mar. 4	Dec. 3	Jan. 2	—
Pensacola	Jan. 26	Feb. 21	Mar. 20	Nov. 8	Nov. 29	Dec. 19
Tallahassee	Feb. 17	Mar. 12	Apr. 5	Oct. 28	Nov. 14	Dec. 2
Tampa	—	Jan. 28	Feb. 25	Dec. 3	Jan. 3	—
GEORGIA						
Albany	Feb. 21	Mar. 12	Mar. 31	Oct. 26	Nov. 13	Dec. 1
Atlanta	Mar. 19	Mar. 28	Apr. 10	Oct. 26	Nov. 8	Nov. 22
Augusta	Mar. 9	Mar. 28	Apr. 15	Oct. 23	Nov. 6	Nov. 20
Brunswick	Jan. 24	Feb. 20	Mar. 18	Nov. 15	Dec. 4	Dec. 24

(*continued*)

getting started

STATE City	Spring (Date) Freeze Probability (Percentage)			Fall (Date) Freeze Probability (Percentage)		
	90	50	10	10	50	90
Columbus	Mar. 3	Mar. 21	Apr. 8	Oct. 27	Nov. 9	Nov. 22
Macon	Feb. 27	Mar. 17	Apr. 4	Oct. 25	Nov. 8	Nov. 22
Savannah	Feb. 17	Mar. 10	Mar. 30	Oct. 31	Nov. 15	Dec. 1
Valdosta	Feb. 22	Mar. 12	Mar. 30	Oct. 27	Nov. 11	Nov. 26
LOUISIANA						
Alexandria	Feb. 12	Mar. 5	Mar. 26	Oct. 30	Nov. 16	Dec. 2
Baton Rouge	Feb. 26	Mar. 15	Apr. 1	Oct. 25	Nov. 10	Nov. 25
Lake Charles	Jan. 23	Feb. 19	Mar. 18	Nov. 6	Nov. 29	Dec. 21
Monroe	Feb. 18	Mar. 9	Mar. 27	Oct. 24	Nov. 7	Nov. 20
New Orleans	Jan. 21	Feb. 20	Mar. 21	Nov. 15	Dec. 5	Dec. 25
Shreveport	Mar. 9	Mar. 21	Apr. 2	Oct. 27	Nov. 10	Nov. 23
MISSISSIPPI						
Columbus	Mar. 11	Mar. 27	Apr. 11	Oct. 15	Oct. 29	Nov. 11
Greenville	Mar. 2	Mar. 18	Apr. 2	Oct. 27	Nov. 12	Nov. 28
Gulfport	Jan. 29	Feb. 22	Mar. 17	Nov. 7	Nov. 26	Dec. 16
Hattiesburg	Mar. 1	Mar. 17	Apr. 3	Oct. 24	Nov. 8	Nov. 23
Jackson	Mar. 12	Mar. 25	Apr. 7	Oct. 14	Oct. 29	Nov. 13
Meridian	Mar. 12	Mar. 27	Apr. 12	Oct. 19	Nov. 3	Nov. 17
Natchez	Feb. 10	Mar. 10	Apr. 7	Oct. 27	Nov. 14	Dec. 2
NORTH CAROLINA						
Asheville	Mar. 28	Apr. 10	Apr. 24	Oct. 11	Oct. 24	Nov. 6
Charlotte	Mar. 18	Apr. 6	Apr. 25	Oct. 14	Nov. 1	Nov. 19
Elizabeth City	Mar. 23	Apr. 6	Apr. 20	Oct. 21	Nov. 4	Nov. 17
Fayetteville	Mar. 18	Apr. 2	Apr. 17	Oct. 20	Oct. 31	Nov. 12
Greensboro	Mar. 31	Apr. 11	Apr. 22	Oct. 14	Oct. 27	Nov. 10
Raleigh-Durham	Mar. 24	Apr. 11	Apr. 29	Oct. 16	Oct. 27	Nov. 7
Wilmington	Feb. 28	Mar. 21	Apr. 12	Oct. 24	Nov. 11	Nov. 29
OKLAHOMA						
Boise City	Apr. 13	Apr. 28	May 12	Oct. 4	Oct. 16	Oct. 29
Enid	Mar. 24	Apr. 4	Apr. 15	Oct. 21	Nov. 3	Nov. 15
Lawton	Mar. 17	Apr. 1	Apr. 15	Oct. 21	Nov. 5	Nov. 19
McAlester	Mar. 19	Mar. 31	Apr. 12	Oct. 15	Oct. 31	Nov. 15
Muskogee	Mar. 21	Apr. 1	Apr. 11	Oct. 19	Nov. 2	Nov. 16
Oklahoma City	Mar. 22	Apr. 6	Apr. 20	Oct. 14	Oct. 27	Nov. 8
Ponca City	Mar. 29	Apr. 13	Apr. 27	Oct. 13	Oct. 26	Nov. 7

STATE / City	Spring (Date) Freeze Probability (Percentage)			Fall (Date) Freeze Probability (Percentage)		
	90	50	10	10	50	90
Stillwater	Mar. 25	Apr. 7	Apr. 19	Oct. 14	Oct. 26	Nov. 17
Tulsa	Mar. 16	Mar. 30	Apr. 13	Oct. 21	Nov. 4	Nov. 17
SOUTH CAROLINA						
Anderson	Mar. 14	Mar. 29	Apr. 13	Oct. 24	Nov. 6	Nov. 20
Charleston	Feb. 27	Mar. 18	Apr. 6	Oct. 30	Nov. 12	Nov. 26
Chester	Mar. 18	Apr. 6	Apr. 25	Oct. 14	Oct. 30	Nov. 15
Columbia	Mar. 19	Mar. 30	Apr. 17	Oct. 16	Nov. 1	Nov. 17
Florence	Mar. 3	Mar. 20	Apr. 5	Oct. 26	Nov. 9	Nov. 23
Georgetown	Feb. 17	Mar. 11	Apr. 2	Nov. 4	Nov. 20	Dec. 6
Spartanburg	Apr. 2	Apr. 14	Apr. 25	Oct. 13	Oct. 29	Nov. 13
TENNESSEE						
Chattanooga	Mar. 23	Apr. 5	Apr. 18	Oct. 19	Nov. 1	Nov. 14
Clarksville	Mar. 29	Apr. 12	Apr. 27	Oct. 8	Oct. 22	Nov. 5
Greensville	Apr. 9	Apr. 23	May 8	Oct. 8	Oct. 20	Oct. 31
Kingport	Apr. 3	Apr. 16	Apr. 29	Oct. 7	Oct. 20	Nov. 2
Knoxville	Mar. 18	Mar. 29	Apr. 9	Oct. 23	Nov. 6	Nov. 20
Memphis	Mar. 8	Mar. 23	Apr. 8	Oct. 27	Nov. 7	Nov. 19
Nashville	Mar. 24	Apr. 5	Apr. 16	Oct. 14	Oct. 29	Nov. 13
Union City	Mar. 23	Apr. 6	Apr. 20	Oct. 6	Oct. 20	Nov. 2
TEXAS						
Abilene	Mar. 10	Mar. 25	Apr. 8	Oct. 28	Nov. 13	Nov. 30
Amarillo	Mar. 29	Apr. 14	Apr. 30	Oct. 14	Oct. 29	Nov. 13
Austin	Feb. 14	Mar. 3	Mar. 21	Nov. 5	Nov. 28	Dec. 21
Beaumont	Jan. 24	Feb. 17	Mar. 16	Nov. 16	Dec. 9	Jan. 1
Brownsville	—	Dec. 31	Feb. 15	Dec. 17	Feb. 2	—
Conroe	Feb. 14	Mar. 5	Mar. 24	Nov. 6	Nov. 25	Dec. 14
Corpus Christi	—	Jan. 25	Feb. 23	Dec. 7	Jan. 11	—
Dallas	Feb. 18	Mar. 16	Apr. 4	Nov. 1	Nov. 20	Dec. 9
El Paso	Feb. 17	Mar. 9	Mar. 29	Oct. 27	Nov. 12	Nov. 29
Fort Worth	Mar. 10	Mar. 26	Apr. 11	Oct. 25	Nov. 11	Nov. 27
Houston	Jan. 20	Feb. 14	Mar. 11	Nov. 18	Dec. 11	Jan. 3
Longview	Feb. 28	Mar. 16	Apr. 2	Oct. 26	Nov. 15	Dec. 2
Lubbock	Mar. 25	Apr. 8	Apr. 22	Oct. 15	Nov. 1	Nov. 17
Midland-Odessa	Mar. 15	Mar. 28	Apr. 11	Oct. 21	Nov. 6	Nov. 23
San Antonio	Feb. 11	Mar. 3	Mar. 23	Nov. 6	Nov. 24	Dec. 11
Waco	Feb. 20	Mar. 12	Mar. 31	Nov. 4	Nov. 24	Dec. 13

more than just nitrogen, phosphorous, and potassium (NPK). They have micronutrients and growth factors we're only beginning to understand. If you embrace the commonsense approach, then you constantly are searching for more organic matter, you use a judicious amount of chemical fertilizer, and you spray only when necessary, using the least toxic, most effective pesticides. In horticultural circles this is referred to as integrated pest management. You'll find soil preparation and managing fertility covered more thoroughly in a later chapter.

CONTAINER GARDENING

The raised beds recommended earlier are really little more than large containers, but let's take it down to a more traditional level: the pot, the barrel, and the basket. Besides being generally much smaller compared with raised beds, they are also portable—handy when you have to move plants in before a hard freeze. They benefit from a loose organic soil mix just like the raised beds, but they dry out quickly, and fertilizer elements leach out rapidly, too. These containers are mostly for vegetables, herbs, and flowers, but some fruits—especially citrus—work well in large pots or barrels.

In most cases, the larger the container, the better. A 15- to 25-gallon pot is a much better size for a tomato plant than a 5-gallon pot. Tomatoes are especially sensitive to uneven moisture: with too much water, because the soil lacks oxygen in this condition, roots aren't able to take up enough water (this usually isn't a problem in containers); with too little water (a more likely problem with containers), you get the same water stress results. Most plants will do fine while they are small, but once they have set fruit, the water demand skyrockets. A large plant may need to be watered two to three times per day, or blossom end rot may develop in the fruit. Also be sure to water thoroughly so that water runs through the drain holes each time. What if you have to go to work and can't be home to water two or three times a day? A drip or microsprinkler watering system set up with a time clock is the best answer. Set the system to come on early in the morning and around noon. When you get home from work, you can water more if necessary.

Need a few fresh herbs close to the kitchen door, but you're not quite ready for a full-blown kitchen garden? Herbs flourish in a hanging basket. Buy a big one—18 to 24 inches in diameter—and fill it with a commercial potting soil. The wire ones with coconut fiber liners look super planted with herbs like thyme, oregano, sweet marjoram, and rosemary to drape over the basket. For a center accent plant, use a clump of chives or a scented geranium.

Nutrients can rapidly leach out of a container's loose soil mix. You can use slow-release fertilizer tablets or encapsulated fertilizer to slow the loss of nutrients, or you can use lots of organic fertilizer that isn't as soluble and more slowly available. Of course, you can also fertilize more often to ensure that adequate nutrients are available. One of the handiest new tools available to the home gardener is the hose-on fertilizer sprayer. You simply hook this device up to your hose, partially fill the container with fertilizer, and turn on the water. It sounds like you would be overdosing the plants with fertilizer salts, but this device proportions fertilizer into the water stream from the saturated solution at the top of the container (after it fills with water). Eventually all of the fertilizer dissolves, and you will need to add more, but there's little danger of burning your plants with too much fertilizer. Fortunately, most soluble home garden fertilizers include a green or blue dye so that you know when the solution is becoming dilute.

Once you have selected the proper container size and have made sure it has enough drain holes to provide adequate drainage, it's important to fill those containers with a good, loose potting mix. Numerous commercial soil mixes are available, or you can mix your own depending on your preference. Try to avoid using excessive amounts of garden soil because these native soils (especially clays) tend to pack up and become hard as a brick over time. If your soil mix is too light, the containers may be unstable. In this case, consider adding sharp sand, fired clay, or haydite to provide additional weight to your soil mix. You can also place a couple of bricks in the bottom of the container to provide additional weight.

Many vegetable, flower, and herb varieties and a few fruits have been especially developed for container gardening. They are generally smaller and more compact, making them better adapted to the confined space of a container. Many urban landscapes are too small or have too much shade for a traditional raised bed kitchen garden. This has resulted in an increased interest in the container garden. Properly planned, a container garden can add real interest and aesthetic beauty to a sunny patio or deck.

Plants in containers aren't necessarily less susceptible to pests. If you use a good potting soil, weeds should be minimal, and soil-borne pests like nematodes and root rot are unlikely problems. The bugs and aboveground diseases, however, will still find your plants. Just be vigilant, and most of these pests can be controlled with low-toxicity organic or biological sprays—especially if you catch them early.

Where do you find a good potting soil? Quality, name brand, bagged soil is great. It usually has been sterilized to eliminate soil pests, and some starter nutrients have been added to make sure your plants aren't stunted from the get-go. However, the honeymoon will be over soon if you don't continually supply the containers with more nutrients. The main drawback to commercial potting soil is the cost. Fill a dozen 30-gallon pots with this stuff, and your garden budget soars. You could buy a garden soil mix by the cubic yard from the local dirt yard, but it usually isn't sterilized, so pests may be more of a concern. Straight compost isn't a bad choice, but this stuff is precious, too. If you can buy good compost by the truckload, then use it in the garden and try filling some pots with it, too. It won't be sterilized, but the good micro-organisms should dominate and ensure a bountiful crop. Good compost has a rich, earthy odor, and the raw materials that went into its manufacture are mostly broken down. Beware of partially decomposed wood chips. They may be dark and rich looking, but if the product is dry and

Gardening through a Child's Eye

Most of us developed our interest in gardening at a very early age. It may have been from a summer spent with our grandmother or grandfather working in their garden. You may have had a mother or father who loved gardening and made sure you helped out with the planting, weeding, and harvesting. You may have even had a neighbor (which happens to be where I think I found my love for gardening) who spent a little extra time showing you the way to plant and care for a garden.

Wherever you learned the joy of gardening, I suspect there was an adult who helped lead the way. It's important that all of us share our knowledge and experiences in the garden with young people. They may complain about the work or having to come outside away from the television or video game, but the experience could result in developing a lifelong hobby with so many benefits that it's hard to place a value on it. Grab the kids or grandkids and haul them out to the garden, kicking and screaming if you must, and show them the wonder and joy of gardening.

looks like shredded fiber, then it's fine for mulch; but if you try to grow in it or mix it with the soil, it will tie up nitrogen for a long time.

Plants in a container often need some type of support. It's no fun to grow a beautiful tomato plant loaded down with fruit and have it blow over in the wind before you can whip up the first salad or BLT (bacon, lettuce, and tomato sandwich—one of the top 10 reasons for gardening). You can support plants with wire tomato cages, wooden trellises staked into the pot, wrought iron plant supports, or whatever your budget and imagination can summon up. Of course, lettuce and other small plants will get by just fine on their own.

Will containers solve all of your garden woes? Probably not, but they do get you in the game quickly with a minimum of heavy labor, and they reduce the pests you will have to contend with. Containers may be your sole venue for gardening, or they can serve as accent plantings in a more traditional kitchen garden.

vegetables

WARM SEASON VEGETABLES

Since the kitchen garden is typically smaller than the old-fashioned truck garden, we're mostly interested in the production of quality vegetables that we really like. Chances are you will find that even with six to eight raised beds you will have plenty to eat fresh, freeze, can, and give to friends. And if you're tempted to try new varieties, it is easy to overproduce a vegetable you like but that you can only eat so much of. Squash, green beans, eggplants, peppers (especially the hot kind), and tomatoes are all likely candidates for this fate. Eventually the neighbors will lock their doors when they see you coming down the street with bags in hand. Actually, it's kind of fun to give produce to unsuspecting recipients—take some to the doctor, the optometrist, and the dentist. Don't forget the post office, other delivery services, restaurants—they're all fair game because the alternative is the compost pile. Most folks will at least take them off your hands and they often rave about the freshness and quality. They rarely discount your bill—make that *never* discount your bill—but that's OK. You've just indoctrinated someone as to how much better "fresh from the garden vegetables" are compared with the store-bought kind.

Many of our warm season vegetables are started early in a greenhouse or cold frame to be transplanted into the garden after spring frosts have passed. Most of us settle for the plants offered at the local nursery, but if you decide to grow your own, be sure to check out the chapter on propagation. At the nursery, plants do sometimes get mixed up; and by the time you realize you have the wrong variety, the season is virtually over, and it is too late to replant.

Warm Season Garden Plans

Seeds and plants for the warm season garden typically go in during March and April. With a bit of luck, you can replant a number of these vegetables again in midsummer for a fall harvest before the first freeze. An ideal plan would include all of the vegetables, herbs, flowers, and fruits that your family loves but that are hard to purchase at the local grocery store. Good candidates include bush beans (especially gourmet varieties like haricot verts and yellow wax beans), cucumbers (grow the burpless or Mediterranean varieties on a trellis), summer squash (think yellow crookneck drizzled with butter and sprinkled with salt and pepper), eggplant (you only need one plant—make it one of the long, skinny, and really tender Asian varieties), peppers (two hybrid bells and one jalapeño [for Willie's Salsa; see recipe]), and lots of tomatoes (three or four medium-sized slicers and two sweet cherry types). What would summer be without fresh basil? Even if you're addicted to pesto, you can only use so much basil. Also include Mexican marigold mint, oregano, and rosemary.

Flowers are not only beautiful; they can attract beneficial insects and butterflies. Zinnias are a must—cosmos, marigolds, gomphrenas, rudbeckias, and many others make the kitchen garden not only a productive place but also a pleasant and enjoyable one.

If you have room for fruit, concentrate on blackberries, peaches, plums, figs, Asian persimmons, and other "easy to grow" varieties.

Asparagus can be very frustrating to grow, especially in the lower South. It just wants to keep growing when it should go dormant. Without dormancy induced by cold weather or withholding irrigation to induce drought, the plants constantly expend energy to grow and don't produce the large spears we expect in the spring. If you decide to try growing asparagus, work up a rich, organic bed with plenty of fertilizer (2–4 pounds per 100 square feet). The vigor of your plants will provide you with the information you need to determine whether you're harvesting for the proper length of time. If the spears developing in the spring and fall continue to get larger in diameter, you can increase the harvest time each season. If they progressively get smaller, cut back on the harvest time in the spring and fall to help improve the vigor of your plants.

Asparagus spears herald spring as they break through the mulch. This perennial is a heavy feeder and it requires constant weeding.

BASIC PLANTING INFORMATION FOR ASPARAGUS

Space between rows (inches)	Seed spacing (inches)	Thin to (inches)	Seed depth (inches)	Days to reach maturity	Comments
36–48	14–18 (crowns)	NA	1–1½	Perennial, begin harvesting second or third year	Can be started from seed but male plants (from divisions) tend to produce more heavily. Fertilize heavily to encourage rapid growth—asparagus is very salt tolerant.

Green beans are a super crop for the kitchen garden. Planted in the spring, they will produce until the heat of summer or until spider mites take them out of production. Plant again the last of August/early September, and they will produce an even more premium crop as the temperatures cool off in the fall. Cooler growing temperatures result in tastier beans. The fall season usually isn't long enough for pole beans, but they're fine in the spring. Virtually any variety will grow well in the South, but for the kitchen garden, concentrate on gourmet varieties like Provider, Festina, Bush Romano, and Maxibel. Green beans are best harvested when they are young and tender, before the seeds begin to swell inside the pod.

BASIC PLANTING INFORMATION FOR BUSH BEANS

Space between rows (inches)	Seed spacing (inches)	Thin to (inches)	Seed depth (inches)	Days to reach maturity	Comments
18–36	2–4	4–6	½–1	45–60	In the spring plant 8–10 weeks after the last freeze. In the fall plant 10–12 weeks before the average first frost. In raised beds plant 6 × 6 to 4 × 8 inches apart.

BASIC PLANTING INFORMATION FOR POLE BEANS

Space between rows (inches)	Seed spacing (inches)	Thin to (inches)	Seed depth (inches)	Days to reach maturity	Comments
36–48	2–4	6	½–1½	50–60	Pole beans are a great way to make use of vertical space in the spring garden. They usually don't have enough time to mature in the fall garden.

the southern kitchen garden

Lima beans take too much room and produce too little in most southern gardens, but the pole varieties like Florida Butter or Carolina Sieva may earn their way when grown on trellises or tepees. Lima beans should be harvested when the seeds are fully developed inside the pod.

BASIC PLANTING INFORMATION FOR POLE LIMA BEANS

Space between rows (inches)	Seed spacing (inches)	Thin to (inches)	Seed depth (inches)	Days to reach maturity	Comments
36–48	4	8–12	1½	75–85	Pole lima beans are your best bet for a good crop of lima beans in the southern kitchen garden. Spring crops only.

Sweet corn is a crop for the truck gardener. You need at least three rows to ensure good pollination, and the plants grow large enough to shade more productive vegetables. That said, a small compact plot—with multiple short rows—of one of the new supersweet corns like Checkered Choice or Mirai is a treat you won't soon forget. Be sure when the silks appear from the developing corn that you shake the tassels (pollen-bearing structures at the top of the corn stalk) to shower the silks with pollen.

It can sometimes be a bit challenging to determine when sweet corn is at its peak. Many gardeners wait until all the silks have turned brown before harvesting. This works for some varieties but certainly not all. Probably the most reliable approach is to feel the ends of the ears to see if the kernels have filled to the end of the ear. You can also puncture the kernels with a fingernail, and if the liquid is milky, that's a good sign for most varieties. Harvest a few ears and taste the corn to see if it's ready to harvest. With our modern sweet corn varieties, you'll find that about 90% of the ears will mature at about the same time.

BASIC PLANTING INFORMATION FOR CORN

Space between rows (inches)	Seed spacing (inches)	Thin to (inches)	Seed depth (inches)	Days to reach maturity	Comments
32–36	2–4	8–12	½–1	70–95	"Sweet gene" varieties need to be isolated from standard varieties to avoid contamination and loss of sweetness. In raised bed gardens, plant seeds 8 inches apart with rows 8–12 inches apart, and include at least three rows in concentrated blocks to ensure pollination.

Cucumbers hanging from a trellis are blemish free and easy to harvest. Best of all they make use of vertical space.

Cucumbers can occupy a lot of space when allowed to trail on the ground, but they are wonderful if trained to grow on a trellis. Concentrate on the quality, high-yielding varieties like the Mediterranean cultivar Oasis, burpless varieties like Sweet Slice, Soo Yoh (Suyo), or go crazy and plant a white cucumber like White Stallion. Pickling varieties are best purchased at the farmers' market since you need a bunch at one time. If you want a few jars of dill slices, there's no reason you can't use any of these varieties. Be sure to harvest daily and remove overripe fruits from the vine, or they will cause the vine to stop producing.

BASIC PLANTING INFORMATION FOR CUCUMBERS

Space between rows (inches)	Seed spacing (inches)	Thin to (inches)	Seed depth (inches)	Days to reach maturity	Comments
48–72	6	12–18 or 3–4 plants per hill	1–1½	50–70	In the kitchen garden, it is usually best to plant on trellises with plants spaced 12 inches apart.

Squashes and pumpkins can take too much room unless you grow on trellises or use bush varieties. Even with a trellis most pumpkins are too heavy. Smaller pumpkins and winter (storing) squash (like acorn, spaghetti, or butternut) can work fine on a trellis. One of our favorites is the climbing zucchini Tromboncino, although this squash can take over the garden. You'll find that you will need to cut it back from other beds—it roots at every node! Actually, it is so smooth and buttery you may be tempted to let it have its way. Bush squash is the best for most kitchen gardens. Yellow crookneck varieties like Dixie or zucchini varieties like Richgreen can be enormously productive in a small bed. Chances are you'll pull them out because you're tired of them and the neighbors are running from you before they stop producing. Summer squash should be harvested when the fruits are small and the skin is tender. Winter squash should be harvested when the fruit is fully mature

Zucchini squash can be amazingly productive. Make sure you have lots of recipes handy and a file of zucchini eaters in mind for the extras. Notice the male and female flowers in this photo— the female flower is at the end of the small zucchini while the male flowers are at the end of a green stem.

and the rind has become tough. You'll find that many of the traditional winter squash are now being harvested and used as summer squash.

BASIC PLANTING INFORMATION FOR SQUASHES AND PUMPKINS

Space between rows (inches)	Seed spacing (inches)	Thin to (inches)	Seed depth (inches)	Days to reach maturity	Comments
24–36 for bush types, 48–72 for trailing types	6–12	24–36 (2–3 plants per hill)	1–2	45–120	Bush varieties will work in the kitchen garden, or plant the trailing types on a trellis to make use of vertical space with 12- to 24-inch spacing.

Cantaloupes and other small melons can be grown on a trellis by tying the fruits when they are about avocado size in a piece of pantyhose. When the melon is fully ripe (referred to as full slip) it will drop loose, blemish free, in the pantyhose.

Melons are a "trellis-only" candidate for most kitchen gardens. If you have a compost pile, consider letting a muskmelon grow up the sides. It will thrive with its roots in the compost. When the melons are baseball size, tie them to the framework with a section of pantyhose—use the toe or tie a knot in one end, slip the melon in, and tie what's left to the compost frame. When the melon "slips" loose from the vine, cut off the hose where it's attached to the frame and throw it over your shoulder. No bugs, no varmints, and it won't even have a flat spot on one side.

Watermelons are a bit more challenging. We recommend queen-size pantyhose. Seedless melons are tempting—just remember you will need a standard variety for pollination, so you will be using a lot of trellis space.

BASIC PLANTING INFORMATION FOR MELONS

Space between rows (inches)	Seed spacing (inches)	Thin to (inches)	Seed depth (inches)	Days to reach maturity	Comments
48–72	6–12 in row, 3–4 seeds per hill	18–24 in row, 2–3 seedlings per hill	½–1	60–90	The only logical way to produce melons, whether they are cantaloupes or small watermelons, in the kitchen garden is to choose small-fruited varieties and grow them on a trellis. When the small melons are baseball size, slip them into a section of pantyhose and tie the hose to the trellis. You'll have beautiful melons without a blemish on them. Hint: For the larger melons choose queen-size pantyhose. Space seedlings 18–24 inches apart on the trellis.

Eggplants rarely make anyone's "Favorite Vegetable" list, probably because of an early childhood experience with a mushy casserole. If you love to grow eggplant but hate to eat them, try slicing them into ¼-inch pieces, then dip the slices in an egg and milk batter, followed by a shake in a plastic bag with Italian bread crumbs. Finally, fry or bake until the

Eggplants

bread crumbs are crisp and sprinkle with Creole seasoning salt. Even picky kids will eat eggplant prepared this way—just don't tell them it's eggplant. Also try blending them in a casserole with Italian cooking sauce, Italian sausage, bread crumbs, and mozzarella, provolone, Romano, and parmesan cheeses. If this bubbly hot treat doesn't convince you to like eggplant, turn to the next vegetable.

Most varieties grow well in the South, but the old Black Beauty variety has a reputation for being bitter when grown under heat and drought stress. The best varieties with thin skins, relatively few seeds, and mild flavor are the long, skinny Asian varieties like Pingtung Long. The green varieties may not look too appetizing, but they "eat good." Try Thai Long Green, Louisiana Long Green, or Harabegan.

Harvesting at the proper time is one of the best ways to eliminate the bitter quality of some eggplant varieties. Eggplant should be harvested when the fruit are still immature, before the seeds begin to harden and the skins are still tender and glossy. Once the skin turns dull and the seeds/flesh begin to turn brown, the fruit is overmature. Also be sure to water and fertilize to encourage rapid growth—this is another key to producing mild-flavored eggplants.

BASIC PLANTING INFORMATION FOR EGGPLANTS

Space between rows (inches)	Seed spacing (inches)	Thin to (inches)	Seed depth (inches)	Days to reach maturity	Comments
24–36	Use transplants	18–30	¼–½-inch seed flats	90	Don't plant until the weather warms up in late March–April or even May in the upper South. Push hard with compost and fertilizer side dressed or applied as a foliar feed. New varieties like Fairy Tale Hybrid AAS and Patio Mohican can be spaced 18 inches apart in the raised bed garden.

Okra would likely be a "miscellaneous vegetable" in most books, but it's hard to leave this vegetable out of a book for the South. Unfortunately, it needs a lot of room to grow. Consider some of the space-saving, dwarf varieties if it seems you don't have room for okra in your garden. In the summer you should be able to buy good-quality okra at a farmers' market, but it doesn't keep well so you may decide to dedicate some space to okra in your kitchen garden. It loves hot weather, so you can plant it after other crops fade in the heat. The velvet varieties like Emerald are primo, but you may also want to try some of the new hybrids like Cajun Delight Hybrid. You might also try growing a few okra plants in a large tub or container. Remember this is a hibiscus relative, and when properly cared for, it makes an attractive flowering plant for the patio. The red hybrid Little Lucy is the perfect size for a container. Be sure to wear a long-sleeved shirt and gloves when harvesting to avoid the itching reaction most gardeners experience from the plant and pods.

Use okra in gumbo if you wish, but the only mouthwatering, toe-curling way to consume okra is fresh and fried. Fried frozen okra is a poor substitute. Cut the okra into ½- to ¾-inch pieces. Mix up an egg-milk batter and pour over the okra (include a couple of diced tomatoes in the mixture to really zing it up), mix thoroughly, and allow the excess batter to settle to the bottom of the container. A handful at a time, shake the okra/tomato pieces in a plastic bag with spicy fish fry (a hot, cornmeal-flour product available at most southern grocery stores). Fry in a single layer in hot peanut oil, turning occasionally until golden brown; then drain on a paper towel and sprinkle with Creole seasoning salt. If this doesn't make your taste buds swoon, then you must be new to the South.

BASIC PLANTING INFORMATION FOR OKRA

Space between rows (inches)	Seed spacing (inches)	Thin to (inches)	Seed depth (inches)	Days to reach maturity	Comments
36–42	4–6	16–24	½–1	48–60	Okra plants are a bit large for some kitchen gardens, but new varieties like Little Lucy (red) and Baby Bubba (green) may save the day. The other choice is to locate a market gardener in your area and buy fresh! Okra seed needs 75°F soil temperatures to germinate, so wait until April/May to plant.

Southern peas including Blackeyes, Purple Hulls, Crowders, and Creams are as southern as it gets. No, they don't have to be fried, but maybe we're missing something here. Usually they are shelled green and cooked—sometimes with green snaps included. Green snaps are the beans with immature peas in them. They can also be harvested dry and stored. Nothing makes "fatback" more useful in the southern kitchen than a "mess" of Blackeyes, Purple Hulls, or Crowders. They are also easy to grow; and being a legume, they make a good "green manure" crop to add nitrogen back to the soil. This is a hot weather vegetable so you must wait until April or May when the soil temperatures are in the 70°F to 85°F range. Look for varieties like Purple Hull Pinkeye, Texas Pinkeye, Mississippi Silver, and Blackeye. Southern peas are usually harvested when the pods are mature and the seeds are fully developed to be used as fresh shelled peas.

BASIC PLANTING INFORMATION FOR SOUTHERN PEAS

Space between rows (inches)	Seed spacing (inches)	Thin to (inches)	Seed depth (inches)	Days to reach maturity	Comments
24–36	2	4–6	1–2	60–70	This is another "space eater" that may not work in most kitchen gardens. Fortunately, this vegetable is often available at farmers' markets from early summer on. If you find an heirloom variety that you must grow, or if you want to try the "yard-long" type beans on a trellis, go with 12- to 18-inch spacing along the trellis.

Bell peppers require heavy fertilization early in the season to promote rapid growth and an early harvest.

Sweet peppers come in a number of forms—bells, sweet cherries, banana, pimento, and Italian Ramshorn. They're all relatively easy to grow, but you can set them out too early— mid-March to early April is usually early enough to plant peppers. Otherwise, they may be stunted by cold temperatures. They also need high fertilization, especially nitrogen. A rich organic soil supplemented with additional nitrogen is the key to early production before it gets too hot. Fortunately, they also come back to produce in the fall if they survive the summer. The biggest and best peppers will come from the first few harvests, and the size will diminish as temperatures heat up; then they will scatter a few peppers through the summer before putting on a big crop in the fall. If you like using colorful (fully ripe) peppers, consider growing some of the smaller-fruited varieties such as sweet cherry, pimento, or Italian Ramshorn. They color much more easily than the large-fruited varieties.

BASIC PLANTING INFORMATION FOR BELL PEPPERS

Space between rows (inches)	Seed spacing (inches)	Thin to (inches)	Seed depth (inches)	Days to reach maturity	Comments
20–36	N/A	Set transplants 18–30	¼	70–100	Peppers can't be planted as early as tomatoes because they are stunted in cold soils, but once they are in the ground (mid-March–April), they need high fertilization. The idea is to grow a quality crop before it gets too hot in the summer. A rich organic soil and foliar feeding on a weekly basis are the keys to this crop. Also be sure to water and mulch to further encourage rapid growth. In raised beds, try a 12 × 18 to 18 × 18 spacing.

the southern kitchen garden

Hot Peppers

Hot peppers are easy to overplant. There are so many interesting ones—even if you plant only one plant of each—you would soon have an acre in hot peppers. Most kitchen gardens can suffice with one jalapeño and one serrano pepper. Occasionally it would be tempting to plant a bed of New Mexico chiles; then sear and freeze a bunch for use later or plant the native chile tepin for hot sauce and the birds. The adventurous may want to plant one jalapeño and a different hot pepper each year. Some peppers like anchos, habaneros, jalapeños, and serranos are becoming readily available in the produce section of larger grocery stores, so it is debatable whether you need to grow them or not.

BASIC PLANTING INFORMATION FOR HOT PEPPERS

Space between rows (inches)	Seed spacing (inches)	Thin to (inches)	Seed depth (inches)	Days to reach maturity	Comments
20–36	N/A	Set transplants 18–30	¼	60–75	Hot peppers are just as susceptible to cold soils as the bell peppers, so hold off until April/May to plant. They also benefit from high fertilization. In raised beds, go with the 12 × 18 or 18 × 18 spacing.

Best Chiles for the Southern Kitchen Garden

Hot peppers are a southern tradition, and they should be included in every southern kitchen garden. Even if you can't stand the heat, you can grow jalapeños such as Señorita, Fooled You, or False Alarm that are almost as sweet as bell peppers and make folks think you're tough.

Most of the hot stuff (capsaicin) is in the placenta or cross walls. Remove it and you can continue the illusion. The really hot ones like habanero may still leave you breathless, and chile pequins may require microsurgery to remove the cross walls.

Aji Dulce	Looks like a habanero, but it's mostly sweet.
Anaheim	This is the pepper that started the green chile craze. New Mexico chiles are super in southern kitchen gardens, too. Look for varieties like Big Jim for a good standard variety, R. Naky if you like 'em mild, Sandia for more spice.
Ancho	A rather spicy top-shaped pepper used for chile rellenos, especially the poblano or fresh green form. Dried anchos are great in chili and stews. Mulato is a brown and hot variation of this pepper.
Chile Pequin	This is the tiny Bird's Eye pepper so popular in vinegar sauce. A must for collard greens.
Habanero	One of the world's hottest peppers! A red variation, Red Savina, may be the hottest at 500,000 Scovill heat units. It has a fruity aftertaste (after you regain consciousness). Try carefully removing the cross walls and seeds before mincing to mix in fresh salsas.
Jalapeño	No self-respecting southerner would plant a garden without at least a couple of jalapeño plants. Even if you go for the mild ones like TAM Mild, Señorita, or False Alarm, try the yellow Jaloro (medium hot) or the Texas-sized Jalapeño Grande (plenty hot) for a little variety.
Serrano	Small, but pretty spicy. The serrano is super for salsa. Real "chileheads" put a few of these with fresh garlic, onion, cilantro, and a bit of seasoned salt in a mini—food processor to make a quick salsa. A teaspoonful in a taco or burrito will turn bland into *Arriba!*

Potatoes like cool weather, but they are also frost sensitive; that's why we plant them very early in the spring about 3 weeks before your average last freeze (Valentine's Day is usually a good time in the lower South) or in late summer (mid-August) for a fall harvest. Potatoes are usually considered a crop for the large garden, but they can be amazingly productive in raised beds, and nothing is easier to store. After digging in late May or November—depending on the planting season—leave them relatively dirty (in other words, don't scrub them), and store them in a dark, cool place. They last a lot longer than store-bought spuds because they haven't been held in storage—ready to burst forth and grow.

If you've never eaten potatoes fresh from the garden, you haven't really eaten potatoes. There's a sweet, fresh quality that has to be experienced to be believed. Good 'ol LaSoda (red) and Kennebec (white) are hard to beat. Fall potatoes are best planted whole from any Ping-Pong ball–sized potatoes you harvested in the spring. Cut up seed potatoes with one to two buds (eyes)—allow them to dry for a couple of days—and then plant these cut potato pieces in the spring. Avoid planting store-bought potatoes—they often have virus diseases.

BASIC PLANTING INFORMATION FOR POTATOES

Space between rows (inches)	Seed spacing (inches)	Thin to (inches)	Seed depth (inches)	Days to reach maturity	Comments
36–42	8–12	N/A	3–4	85–110	Potatoes are usually portrayed as a crop for the large garden, but "fresh from the garden potatoes" are a treat that shouldn't be missed. There's a wholesome sweetness to fresh potatoes that even a kitchen gardener with a few small raised beds should experience. Plant around Valentine's Day, and harvest in May. With a loose organic soil, you can probably dig around and steal a few even earlier. Cut seed potatoes into 2- to 4-ounce pieces and allow them to dry for 2–4 days before planting. In raised beds, use a 12 × 12 to 18 × 18 inch spacing.

Tomatoes are a major passion for many gardeners, and even nonvegetable gardeners often find a place for a couple of tomato plants in the flower beds. It's extremely important to plant varieties that are scrumptious and well adapted to the area. The scrumptious factor you'll have to determine for yourself. For example, some people like a mild tomato—they should be happy with what they can buy at the grocery store. The rest of us want intense flavor and lots of it. Flavor to carry a BLT, top a ¼-pound hamburger . . . flavor that will add zing to a salad . . . acidity, sweetness, and a complex tomatoness too complicated to describe. Tomato lovers know a good tomato—juicy ripe from the vine and warm, or at least at room temperature. Refrigeration kills the flavor of a good tomato.

The best varieties are usually modern hybrids. Heirlooms are fun to grow, and some are quite tasty, but they usually have some defect that led to their demise. Odd shapes, taste, and texture are sometimes to blame, but often it is susceptibility to disease pests that caused them to fall from favor. Quite simply, *heirloom* and *loser* are synonyms. Plant a few varieties like German Johnson, Persimmon, Georgia Streak, Jaune Flamme, and Cherokee Purple each year for the fun and variety of it, but concentrate on the good hybrid varieties.

Cherry tomatoes are the easiest of all tomatoes to grow, and they will continue to produce even during the heat of summer. Gardener's Delight, Sweet 100, Porter, and Sweet Chelsea are some of the best. Texas Wild is a tiny tomato with big taste. Unfortunately, the plant is likely to cover your kitchen garden, the kitchen, and your house if the season is long enough.

BASIC PLANTING INFORMATION FOR TOMATOES

Space between rows (inches)	Seed spacing (inches)	Thin to (inches)	Seed depth (inches)	Days to reach maturity	Comments
36–48	N/A	Use transplants at 24–42 inches.	¼	65–90	Start seeds in a greenhouse or frame in January for early spring transplants (February/March). You can start tomatoes indoors under fluorescent lights, but be sure to place the seed flats close (2–6 inches) to the bulbs, or they will be "leggy." In the spring, set out transplants on the average last frost date to 8 weeks later. In the fall, it's best to concentrate on early-maturing varieties like the cherries since tomatoes are slow to ripen as the days grow short and cool.

the southern kitchen garden

Willie's Salsa

One day during tomato season (the plump, juicy, red things were lying all over the counter), I decided it was time to create my own version of the fresh salsas I had enjoyed at Tex-Mex restaurants. I started chopping tomatoes, onions, jalapeños, cilantro, and garlic. I'd chop, then add a dash of Creole seasoned salt, chop some more, add more seasoned salt and some black pepper, then some fresh lime juice. Before I knew it, the stuff started to taste pretty good. After a few hours in the fridge, it was even better. The garlic sorta knocked your head off, but as long as everyone ate some, no one seemed to mind.

4–6 regular tomatoes or 6–8 Roma type
　　tomatoes
½–1 Texas SuperSweet or 1015 onion
Juice of 1 lime
1 tbsp. Creole seasoning salt
1 tsp. coarse black pepper
1–2 jalapeños (serranos or similar hot peppers)
1–2 cloves of fresh garlic (*do not substitute*)
1–2 fistfuls of fresh cilantro (*do not substitute or omit*)

Begin by chopping the tomatoes into fine pieces. The Romas make a drier salsa, but they aren't as flavorful, either (in the winter/football season, they're about the only decent choice). You'll need a supersharp knife for this job. I make cuts from the blossom end, about ¼ inch apart, then turn the fruit 90° and make similar cuts. Finally, cut crossways to get small rectangular pieces. Do the same with the onion, or use your Vegematic. Combine tomatoes and onions in a bowl; then squeeze the lime juice over both, and add the seasoning salt and pepper. Mince the peppers and garlic, or try chopping them in a small food processor. Stir all of this together.

Wash the cilantro thoroughly. It's hard to get good cilantro in the summer when you need it for salsa, but you have to have it. I like to remove most of the stems, and chop it into fine pieces—unidentified, black yucky pieces can come out, too. This is the most tedious part of the job, but it is essential. Stir again and put in the refrigerator to allow the flavors to blend. Expect the salsa to taste hotter with time, as more of the capsaicin diffuses out of the peppers. Tomatoes taste best at room temperature, but don't get careless—even though this salsa has a lot of acidity, it shouldn't be left out of the refrigerator for more than a few hours—or one football game/ice skating championship.

For a little variety, try adding ¼ to ½ tsp. chipotle powder or cinnamon.

Willie's Salsa is a great way to use those homegrown tomatoes and jalapeños. The rest of the ingredients like garlic, limes, onion, and cilantro you may have to pick up at the store since they are often out of season when the tomatoes ripen.

Miscellaneous warm season vegetables adapted to the kitchen garden are varied, and a number are covered in our sections on specialty gardens. Some others you might want to consider include **climbing spinach,** also called Malabar spinach. This is a gorgeous, vining plant with shiny green, heart-shaped leaves that tastes a lot like spinach. The texture is a little slick, but mixed with store-bought lettuce (we're talking midsummer here) and other salad vegetables, the flavor is a great addition to a salad. **Purslane** is a weed, but it is also quite good in a salad, and since you're pulling it anyway, why not take some to the kitchen? If nature doesn't provide it free of charge, you can order seed of selected varieties. **Sunroots** are the underground tubers of a native sunflower. They could easily fill in for the summer, and by fall they will not only produce tubers but also have small but pretty flowers. When you dig them, be sure to clean them and place them in the refrigerator in a plastic bag. They can quickly go limp and they don't revive. If you don't need the space for a fall crop leave them in place and dig the tubers as needed.

Tomatillos are a must-have in the Tex-Mex garden, but they lend themselves to any kitchen garden with a bit of space left after the spring crop of potatoes or beans fizzles out in the heat. You can even direct sow them in early summer and thin them to a 12- to 18-inch spacing—since you probably can't find transplants, anyway. They thrive in the heat, and before you know it you'll be spreading *verde* sauce on everything. Try the Toma Verde variety.

Yard-Long Beans are a staple in the Asian garden, but they are related to our southern peas so they, too, can be a hot weather crop for an empty trellis. Pick them when 12 to 18 inches, and use them like green "snaps" in a stir-fry or a traditional southern pea recipe.

COOL SEASON VEGETABLES

Getting ready for the fall garden can be a chore. To start with, many cool season vegetables need to be planted before the warm season crops have finished in September, October, and even into early November. So you end up with a row of bush beans next to the broccoli, or you're trying to coax a few tomatoes along before the first hard freeze—and you would really like to have the space for sugar snap peas or something. Finally, the freeze hits and you're faced with a garden half brown and ugly and a few cool season crops struggling back after the freeze. Well, you just have to get brutal and start pulling out the dead stuff—often you'll have to replant marginally hardy crops like newly sprouted radishes, small lettuce plants, chard, and the like. Our mild winters are a blessing, but we do have the occasional freeze. Thirty-two degrees or slightly below isn't a problem, but temperatures in the mid-20s are more damaging.

Also don't forget to fertilize. Most cool season crops are heavy feeders—especially the onion family and greens. This does put you between a rock and a hard place because vigorous plants are more susceptible to cold weather, but it's worth the risk;

and if you have to, just replant. Foliar feeding is your best bet. Hook up one of the fertilizer sprayers to the hose, fill it with soluble fertilizer, and soak the garden down. Some nutrients will be absorbed by the foliage, and the rest will be available through the soil. Of course, you can also side dress with granular fertilizer—if possible, look for the nitrate form (potassium nitrate or ammonium nitrate) of fertilizer as nitrates are more readily taken up in cold soils compared with fertilizers that only contain ammonium nitrogen.

Keep the frost protection handy. Covering your less hardy crops or tender seedlings on one or two occasions per year is usually all it takes to ensure a tremendous cool season garden. Remember you will need a good insulator to retain enough ground heat to protect tender plants—a single layer of clear plastic won't get the job done. It can even be colder under this type of covering. First use an old blanket or a commercial product like Frost Blanket; then you can cover this with plastic to protect from the wind. Most plastic greenhouses have a double layer of plastic (thus benefiting from the dead air space insulation), and, of course, these structures also have heaters running inside.

You may even have a few weeds and bugs, but they are easy to control. Early in the fall leaf-shredding beetles and their larvae—for example flea beetles or yellow-margined beetles—can wreck a crop of mustard or other greens, but spray early with low-toxicity pesticides like rotenone, spinosad, or neem oil or just turn under the crop and start over. Aphids can sometimes be persistent, but high-pressure water sprays will often reduce the numbers enough that the predators and parasites like lady beetles and tiny wasps will keep them in check. Also treat the yard around the garden for fire ants—they protect and farm the aphids for the honey-dew exudates, so aphids can really get out of hand with fire ants to scare off the predators/parasites.

Home Mushroom Production

This crop may seem a bit complicated and technical for most gardeners, but since kitchen gardeners are impassioned by the quality and variety of their gardens, it really isn't too high to reach. Fortunately, there are specialty sources for substrates, mushroom spawn, books, and all the supplies you could ever need should you decide to start from scratch to grow your own mushrooms. Beginners and the occasional mushroom enthusiast can even purchase kits that are ready to incubate for a delicious crop of home-grown mushrooms (look in the seed catalog list). Shiitakes, oyster mushrooms, Lion's Mane (*Hericium*), portobellos, and more are just a few weeks/months away, and they can be grown in an out-of-the-way place where you couldn't garden very successfully anyway. In fact, many of the mushroom species require cool temperatures so you may be producing them in the kitchen instead of in the kitchen garden. During the winter, they may thrive in the garage or a storage building with a minimum of heat.

Cool Season Garden Plans

The cool season garden is easier to cultivate in a number of ways. The insects, diseases, and weeds aren't as numerous, but getting started in the heat of late summer/fall is sometimes a challenge. Use fiber row cover or whatever shade it takes to get your plants started in the fall, and expect to reap a bountiful harvest most of the fall, winter, and early spring. Bush beans are a warm season crop, but they can be planted in late August/September to mature during cooler weather in October and November—they're even better than the spring crop. Snow peas can be planted in late August—they don't like this weather, but they will germinate and survive until cooler weather arrives and then produce a bumper crop. In late September/October, you can begin to seed crops like lettuce, beets, onions, radishes, spinach, Swiss chard, mustard, kale, collards, and carrots—or if you like, set out lettuce transplants. About the same time, set out broccoli, cauliflower, and Chinese cabbage transplants—try a second crop of broccoli in January, but the others (especially cauliflower and Chinese cabbage) tend to bolt to seed in the spring. One or two celery plants should suffice since you can harvest a few outer stems as needed and keep the plants going all winter. In the herb garden, plant chives, cilantro, dill, parsley, savory, thyme, garlic, and arugula. Flowers for the cool season garden could include dianthus (pinks and carnations), violas, pansies, snapdragons, nigella, agrostemma (corncockle), and bread seed poppies.

One of the most difficult considerations in the kitchen garden is "What to leave in and what to take out?" Warm season crops may still be producing when you would like to plant cool season crops. Come spring and you have the same problem with cool season crops like dill that you would like to leave in for a while, but it is time to plant the bush beans. There's no easy solution to these dilemmas; you just have to decide which crop is being the most productive, the most appreciated by the family, and whether the succeeding crop can be expected to be productive if its planting is delayed. These are minor frustrations compared to those you probably encounter in your 9–5 day job. Remember, gardening is supposed to be fun!

the southern kitchen garden

Beets aren't likely to find their way into many kitchen gardens unless, of course, you're a fan of beet greens. Then the crop begins to make more sense. The beet root by itself is best in a larger garden and even then, not that many folks really crave beets. Newer varieties like Scarlet Supreme, Red Ace, and Merlin are great microwaved with butter, but most people forget to cook the greens. They are very mild—they're related to chard—and cooked with a bit of bacon, a little vinegar, and salt, they're quite good. The tender young greens are often used in salads.

Beets

BASIC PLANTING INFORMATION FOR BEETS

Space between rows (inches)	Seed spacing (inches)	Thin to (inches)	Seed depth (inches)	Days to reach maturity	Comments
14–24	1	3–5	¼–½	50–65	Don't be surprised if it seems like each seed comes up twice—most beet varieties are polyembryonic (more than one plant per seed). In raised beds, try a spacing of 3 × 3 to 3 × 5.

vegetables

Carrots fresh from the garden are a treat to munch on while you work in the garden and they are oh so much sweeter than the store-bought variety. Bring them to the table after a few minutes in the microwave with a little butter or get fancy and try Debbi's Carrot Soufflé.

Carrots from the grocery store aren't too bad, but it's easy to find space in the kitchen garden to tuck a row of carrots in between the radishes, turnips, or collards. And there are some exciting new varieties like purple carrots—Purple Haze—white carrots—Lunar White—and carrots with extra carotene and sweetness like Mokum or Pot O' Gold. Carrots need a loose, organic soil with balanced nutrition. How many times have you heard some "radio guy" tell a caller to add more phosphorous to ensure good production of carrots, radishes, and so forth? This explanation is a bit oversimplified. Carrots need all the essential elements in a well-balanced, fertile soil. They also need to be thinned 1 to 2 inches apart to give the roots enough room to develop. Ruthless thinning is the mark of an experienced gardener!

BASIC PLANTING INFORMATION FOR CARROTS

Space between rows (inches)	Seed spacing (inches)	Thin to (inches)	Seed depth (inches)	Days to reach maturity	Comments
14–24	¼–½	1–2	Rake lightly into surface.	70–80	Be careful not to plant too deep, and be ruthless at thinning within 2 weeks of germination. In raised beds, try broadcast sowing and thinning to 1 × 1 or 2 × 2 depending on the variety.

Debbi's Carrot Soufflé

1 lb. of carrots

½ cup (1 stick) butter, melted

3 eggs

1 cup sugar

3 tbsp. flour

1 tsp. baking soda

1 tsp. vanilla

Peel, slice, and steam the carrots until soft. Drain, put in blender with melted butter and blend. Add remaining ingredients and blend until smooth. Pour into a 1 ½-quart, lightly greased casserole dish. Bake 45 minutes (or longer) until firm in a 350° oven. This dish tastes more like a dessert than a vegetable dish. So don't be surprised to hear your kids begging for more carrots.

Celery is readily available at the store and the quality is OK. However, nothing is more frustrating than to have a nice bunch of celery go bad in the refrigerator because you only needed a few stalks 2 weeks ago. The kitchen gardener only needs a plant or two, and it is easy to have it thrive from fall to early spring in the garden. Even though the grocery store celery is adequate, fresh is always better, and it's easy to harvest a few outer stalks of celery right from the garden. The various Utah and Florida strains are fine, but there is also cutting celery, Afina, which produces lots of small stems with more intense flavor. If you're really adventurous, you could just go crazy and plant red celery.

You don't need to plant a lot of celery—one or two plants should be enough because you can just harvest a few stems at a time as the need arises. Just think. No more limp celery stalks that have been hiding in the hydrator for two months.

BASIC PLANTING INFORMATION FOR CELERY

Space between rows (inches)	Seed spacing (inches)	Thin to (inches)	Seed depth (inches)	Days to reach maturity	Comments
24–36	Use transplants	6–10	¼	80–105	This is an easy vegetable to grow in the fall/winter garden, and it is pretty enough to plant in a flower bed. If you really want "pretty," plant one of the red celeries like Redventure. Any of the celery varieties can be harvested a stalk or two at a time, or plant one of the bunching celeries like Dinant or Afina to cut for seasoning.

vegetables

Chard (Swiss chard) is one of the easiest leafy vegetables to grow. It is mild, delicious, and beautiful in the garden. Essentially it is a beet that is grown for its leaves and leaf petioles rather than for roots. New varieties like Bright Lights AAS come in spectacular colors with red, yellow, orange, and pink petioles—they could fit in a flower arrangement just as easily as in a salad bowl at the dinner table.

BASIC PLANTING INFORMATION FOR CHARD

Space between rows (inches)	Seed spacing (inches)	Thin to (inches)	Seed depth (inches)	Days to reach maturity	Comments
18–30	2–3	6–8	½	50–60	Chard is relatively easy to grow. It needs plenty of nitrogen, and unlike most vegetables, it will thrive in a neutral to alkaline pH soil. Unfortunately, it won't survive a hard freeze without some protection. Usually it only takes one or two coverings per winter to bring it through. If you lose it, plant again about 2 weeks before the average last frost date in the spring, and it should produce before the heat of summer. In raised beds, space 6 × 6 to 8 × 8.

The **cabbage** family includes most of our favorite cool season vegetables. Cauliflower, broccoli, brussels sprouts, kohlrabi, collards, kale, mustard, turnips, and radishes all belong in the crucifer family. A number of Asian vegetables like Chinese cabbage could also be added to the list. With the long cool season we enjoy in the South, it's easy to have these vegetables fresh from October to June. Even in the summer we can enjoy frozen broccoli, cauliflower, and more. For the earliest harvest, you will need to start the seed for transplants as soon as late July. Then set the small plants (you may also be able to buy them at the local nursery) in September. Continue planting through the fall even though a hard freeze could short-circuit your efforts. The plants in this family that produce an edible flower head like cauliflower and broccoli are rather susceptible to a freeze so, if a "Norther" blows in, plan to harvest all flowering shoots. The plants in this family are heavy feeders. They need plenty of fertilizer, especially nitrogen. Work lots of compost into the soil and foliar feed, if necessary, to ensure rapid growth.

Cabbage is really a vegetable for the large garden and the grocery store quality is not all that bad. Still, it's a pretty plant and a few cabbage sets of Early Jersey Wakefield (an heirloom) or one of the red-leaf varieties or the crinkled-leaf Savoy types look good even in a flower bed.

Cabbage seems to cry out for a big garden but who says you have to plant a whole row. Plant one or two just to prove you can and make the best coleslaw your family has ever eaten!

BASIC PLANTING INFORMATION FOR CABBAGE

Space between rows (inches)	Seed spacing (inches)	Thin to (inches)	Seed depth (inches)	Days to reach maturity	Comments
24–48	3–4 or use transplants	18–24	¼–½	60–120	Fresh cabbage is really not bad from the grocery store, and it takes a lot of space to grow it yourself. Try the early hybrids or an heirloom like Jersey Wakefield. Plant a red cabbage like Sombrero just because it is pretty.

Broccoli

Broccoli is a favorite vegetable with most gardeners—and their kids, surprisingly, who especially like it with a cheese sauce. Green Comet/Southern Comet and Packman have been standards in kitchen gardens for years because they produce lots of side shoots. A new variety, Gypsy Hybrid, is truly outstanding though. It has the side shoots but it also has a sweet flavor that makes it a hit at the table.

BASIC PLANTING INFORMATION FOR BROCCOLI

Space between rows (inches)	Seed spacing (inches)	Thin to (inches)	Seed depth (inches)	Days to reach maturity	Comments
24–36	4–6 or use transplants	18–24	¼–½	55–80	Broccoli can be planted as early as September in the fall and again in January/February for a spring crop. The fall crop will benefit from the use of fiber row cover to protect it from heat and drying winds. The spring crop may need the heavier "frost blanket" to protect tender seedlings from late frosts. Try a raised bed spacing of 18 × 18.

the southern kitchen garden

A harvest of cauliflower like this is easy in the fall garden. Modern hybrids like Snow Crown and White Cloud are easy to grow. For a little variety plant the neon purple Graffiti or Panther green cauliflower.

Cauliflower takes a bit of space, but it's worth it for some of the new varieties. Green cauliflower like the variety Alverda or the purple Violet Queen cauliflowers (sometimes referred to as a broccoli) are so strikingly beautiful and tasty that they deserve a bit of space in the kitchen garden. They also don't need to be blanched like most of the white varieties. Blanching cauliflower is a fairly common practice. By blanching the developing curd, you exclude light, which inhibits the development of pigments that cause the head to develop off-color. This process involves pulling up the outer green leaves over the curd when it's approximately 2 to 3 inches in diameter and tying them to keep the cauliflower pure and white. It's a good idea to unwrap the leaves periodically to check the head for insect damage.

BASIC PLANTING INFORMATION FOR CAULIFLOWER

Space between rows (inches)	Seed spacing (inches)	Thin to (inches)	Seed depth (inches)	Days to reach maturity	Comments
24–48	Use transplants	24	¼–½	50–75	Cauliflower is best planted in the fall 6–8 weeks before the average first freeze. Spring plantings have a tendency to bolt to seed too soon. Use a raised bed spacing of 24 × 24.

Brussels sprouts are so different fresh from the garden. Instead of being strong, even bitter tasting, they are sweet and delicious—ready to soak up fresh butter, some salt, and pepper. Definitely go for the modern hybrids like Jade Cross and Oliver. They are more vigorous, plus they produce better sprouts sooner than open pollinated varieties. Removal of the lower leaves is not necessary, but once the plants have grown to 18 to 24 inches in height breaking out the terminal bud will speed up the production of side buds (sprouts).

BASIC PLANTING INFORMATION FOR BRUSSELS SPROUTS

Space between rows (inches)	Seed spacing (inches)	Thin to (inches)	Seed depth (inches)	Days to reach maturity	Comments
24–36	Use transplants	12–18	¼–½	85–110	Brussels sprouts are attractive enough to include in the flower border. Be sure to use modern hybrids—they tend to produce sprouts without as much tending. Fertilize heavily to further encourage side sprouts.

Collards, kale, and kohlrabi are the other close relatives of the wild cabbage. Collards and mustard are the most popular greens crops in the South, while kale—basically a collard with frilly leaves—is more popular in the North. Kohlrabi is their strange cousin with its swollen stem that tastes like a mild, sweet turnip. In fact, once you try kohlrabi, you may never eat another turnip. Of course, you can eat the leaves of any of these cabbage relatives, so why not just grow kohlrabi? The main reason is—if you're after greens, kohlrabi just doesn't produce as much foliage, and the flavor may not be as good. The beauty of kale and collards is that you can harvest leaves from the bottom up, and the plants just keep producing until the heat makes them tougher and less sweet.

BASIC PLANTING INFORMATION FOR COLLARDS, KALE, AND KOHLRABI

Space between rows (inches)	Seed spacing (inches)	Thin to (inches)	Seed depth (inches)	Days to reach maturity	Comments
18–36	3–4 inches or use transplants	8–12	¼–½	50–75	There's no excuse for not having greens all winter and into early summer. These plants are hardy, and they seem to get sweeter with cool weather. Space plants 6 × 6 to 12 × 12 in raised beds, and harvest the lower leaves as needed. Kohlrabi is a smaller plant and can be spaced 4 × 4.

the southern kitchen garden

Mustard and turnips have a rougher leaf surface, but they are still in the cabbage family. Both are prized for their leaves cooked with some chopped bacon, green onions, and cider vinegar. And some folks even eat the turnip roots. No doubt, it's an "acquired taste" fostered partly through custom and partly as a result of the Great Depression. The big Purple-Top White Globe turnips are what the old folks filled their bellies with, but the small Asian turnips are even sweeter and mature about as fast as a radish (30–45 days). The young, tender foliage of any turnip variety is great for greens, but there are varieties that don't form much of a root that are even better for that purpose. Mustard greens along with collard greens are two of the main ingredients that define soul food. You won't be far off if you prepare the two (they're good mixed) as suggested at the beginning of this paragraph, and sprinkle on some black pepper and Creole seasoning salt.

Turnips

BASIC PLANTING INFORMATION FOR MUSTARD AND TURNIPS

Space between rows (inches)	Seed spacing (inches)	Thin to (inches)	Seed depth (inches)	Days to reach maturity	Comments
18–24	1	3–4	¼–½	30–55	More greens! Turnips also produce roots. Try broadcasting these vegetables in raised beds, and thin them to a 4 × 4 to 4 × 6 spacing.

Radishes are a snap in the cool season garden. In fact they should be ready in about a month after planting. Be sure to thin them immediately after germination to one inch apart and grow them in a rich, organic soil.

Radishes are fun and easy to grow. They're a great crop to get the kids involved with because they come up immediately, mature rapidly, and they're pretty. Unfortunately, they taste like radishes. Oh, well, put them in a salad—or better yet—let the kids help make the salad and badda bing, you've tricked them into eating a vegetable. A habit they're likely to reject without a lot of tricking, but that's the beauty of a kitchen garden: it's close at hand and hard to ignore. Should you spark some interest in horticulture, you may be grooming the next Luther Burbank. Then you can announce to all your friends that your son or daughter is a "plant breeder." Some will stare, most will ignore you, and a few might even wonder what you're talking about. Who knows—your offspring might develop the World's Most Beautiful and Easy to Care for Rose, a new food crop that will feed the hungry, or "Worst Case Scenario"—a new radish.

BASIC PLANTING INFORMATION FOR RADISHES

Space between rows (inches)	Seed spacing (inches)	Thin to (inches)	Seed depth (inches)	Days to reach maturity	Comments
18–24	½	1–2	¼–½	25–30	Plant up to 3 months before the average first fall frost and for 4–6 weeks after the average spring frost date. Sowing a row every few weeks could keep you in radishes 6–8 months out of the year. Be sure to thin early—as soon as the seedlings emerge—to promote good root formation. In raised beds, try broadcasting the seed and thinning to 2 × 2 for little radishes and 4 × 4 to 6 × 6 for large radishes like daikon.

Garlic

Garlic is a member of the onion family, and like the rest of the family, it prefers cold weather. The softneck varieties (artichoke and silverskin types) are the best for the southern kitchen garden, and they happen to be the ones you will most likely see at the store. The hardneck varieties should also do well in the upper South. Garlic is easy to grow—just break up a bulb into cloves and plant them about an inch deep in the fall, then expect to see what looks like an ugly crop of stunted corn stalks all winter long. Come spring you'll be ready to dig them up and clean them into individual cloves and freeze them in freezer jars (plastic bags won't contain their powerful flavors). They don't store well hanging in a shed during our hot, wet summers. Garlic can be harvested at any stage. Even the green leaves can be cut and brought in the kitchen for use—some cooks even rave about the tender, mild roots of the garlic plant used fresh from the garden. Allow the necks to dry and fall over before digging the bulbs to store for the kitchen or to plant next season.

BASIC PLANTING INFORMATION FOR GARLIC

Space between rows (inches)	Seed spacing (inches)	Thin to (inches)	Seed depth (inches)	Days to reach maturity	Comments
12–24	Cloves 2 inches apart	4–6	Cover tip ½ inch	120–160	Set cloves in October/November. Use a raised bed spacing of 4 × 4 inches.

Lettuces are one of the easiest of all the cool season crops to grow. Just remember to concentrate on the leaf lettuce varieties and don't plant the seed too deep. The seed is small and needs light to germinate. Lightly rake it into the soil, and keep the soil moist until it germinates. Lettuce seed also doesn't store well—even with cold, dry storage—it may only be good for 2 to 3 years, so it is not impossible that you may plant seed that doesn't have much germination potential. If it's not up in a week, replant or head to the nursery for a flat of lettuce transplants. Almost any leaf lettuce or romaine will thrive in the southern kitchen garden. Be sure to cover the plants if a freeze much below 32° is predicted (especially if the plants are conditioned to warm winter days), and water and fertilize often. Hardened-off plants (grown on the dry side with cooler temperatures) can handle much colder temperatures approaching the mid-20s. Some winters you may lose a crop, but replant after the severe weather passes, and in a month or less you'll be back in business. Many gardeners find that leaf lettuce harvested directly from the garden has a bitter flavor. If you refrigerate the lettuce for a few days prior to use, you'll find that this bitterness will go away.

BASIC PLANTING INFORMATION FOR LETTUCE

Space between rows (inches)	Seed spacing (inches)	Thin to (inches)	Seed depth (inches)	Days to reach maturity	Comments
12–24	½–1	8–12	Lightly cover	40–90	Tiny lettuce seeds need light to germinate. If you have trouble getting them to come up, try just sprinkling them on the surface and watering them in—be sure to keep the soil moist until they germinate. You may want to try covering the seedbeds with row cover to retain moisture and enhance germination. Lettuce transplants are readily available if you have trouble with seeds. Lettuce seed also doesn't keep very long, so you may occasionally get a bad batch of seed. Space 6 × 6 to 8 × 8 inches in raised beds.

the southern kitchen garden

Garden (English) and edible podded peas are difficult to grow but they are oh-so-rewarding when things go right. In fact, edible podded peas are the candy of the fall and winter garden. You'll find that very few of them ever make it to the kitchen. They won't produce in the heat of summer, but you can start them as early as August for fall production. A hard freeze will knock them out, but cover them the best you can with a good insulator, and they will thrive throughout most of the weather we have in the winter. A second crop can be planted in January for early spring production—expect rain and hot weather to bring on the powdery mildew, but don't try to spray; just consider the season over. While you can grow garden peas (the kind you have to shell), and they are won-

Peas

derful fresh from the garden, the sugar snap and super sugar snap peas that give you an edible pod (you still have to string it) with a full-size pea inside seem like a better deal. The plants are also quite vigorous and need a good trellis for support.

BASIC PLANTING INFORMATION FOR GARDEN PEAS AND EDIBLE PODDED PEAS

Space between rows (inches)	Seed spacing (inches)	Thin to (inches)	Seed depth (inches)	Days to reach maturity	Comments
24–36	1–2	2–3	1	50–70	Plant early in August for a fall crop and in January for a spring crop. Fiber row cover may be needed to protect tender seedlings from heat/drying wind in the fall and frost blanket to protect from late frosts in the winter. The best way to grow this crop in the kitchen garden is on a trellis to make use of vertical space. Space plants 2–4 inches along the trellis.

Spinach

Spinach thrives in cool weather and short days, but it is also demanding in that spinach requires a deep, loamy soil and plenty of fertilizer—especially nitrogen. It is also one of the few vegetables that likes a neutral to slightly alkaline soil so be sure to check the pH and if necessary, lime the soil to achieve a pH of 7.0 or higher. Using calcium nitrate fertilizer to side-dress the spinach row is also a good idea. Be sure to thin the plants 3 to 5 inches apart in the row, and foliar feed or side-dress often to keep the plants growing actively.

BASIC PLANTING INFORMATION FOR SPINACH

Space between rows (inches)	Seed spacing (inches)	Thin to (inches)	Seed depth (inches)	Days to reach maturity	Comments
14–18	1	3–5	½–¾	45–60	This is one of the few vegetables that thrive in a neutral to alkaline pH (7.0–7.5) soil. It is also strictly a fall crop since it bolts to seed quickly in the spring. Use a raised bed spacing of 5 × 5 inches.

Onions are a cinch in the cool season garden if you plant the right varieties at the right time. For most of the South it is important to plant short-day varieties. Onions planted from seed in the fall (October/November) come up and grow through a cool/moist period called *vernalization* that prepares them to produce bulbs in response to lengthening days in the spring. Short-day onions respond to a shorter, long day and make this response in time to mature bulbs before we get into hot weather. Intermediate-day and long-day onions don't get the signal in time (it's already too hot), or the days never get long enough to initiate the bulbing response. A relatively new category—Day Neutral onions—are also worth a try in southern kitchen gardens. Most gardeners will find that planting short-day onion transplants (like Grano, 1015, Texas SuperSweet, Burgundy) in January is

Short-day onions like these Texas SuperSweets are easy to grow in the Southern garden. Seed needs to be planted from mid-October to early November and seedlings spaced out in early January. Resist the urge to set out plants in the fall as they often bolt to seed.

the easiest way to ensure a good crop of sweet, mild short-day onions. Don't forget the multiplying onions like Evergreen White Bunching or Iwatasuki (multiplier #9) or Louisiana Multiplying Shallots. Regular French shallots are a bust because they don't get the response to bulb soon enough and usually rot in the garden as the heat and rainfall picks up in early summer. Gardeners in the upper South may do alright with them, however. They can also grow the intermediate-day onions like Sweet Spanish and Bermuda.

BASIC PLANTING INFORMATION FOR ONIONS

Space between rows (inches)	Seed spacing (inches)	Thin to (inches)	Seed depth (inches)	Days to reach maturity	Comments
12–24	½	4–6	¼–½	95–160	Bulbing onions should be planted from seed in the fall—September/November. You can also set out transplants in January/February or simply thin out and move the seedlings you planted earlier. A 4 × 4 inch spacing should work fine in raised beds.

Cool Season Gourmet Vegetables

The cool season is a grand time to add the exotic to your kitchen garden and to your diet. One obvious angle to take is planting vegetables in different colors. Beets come in golden yellow, white, or red and white striped. Not all broccolis are green; the variety Violet Queen is a beautiful violet/purple. Not all cauliflowers are white, either. Look for orange Cheddar, green as in Panther, neon purple Graffiti, or try the hybrid broccoflower for a green, brocco-cauliflower-looking thing. Purple cabbage (also referred to as red) isn't that new, but it does hint that the purple gene is there, and it could end up in any of the cabbage relatives—there's even a purple brussels sprouts, though it's not very vigorous.

Think all carrots are orange? Not hardly. They also come in white, yellow, and the latest and best-tasting color—purple. Purple carrots may be the ugliest vegetable in the garden, but they look gorgeous sliced and diced for the table, and they're sweeter, with less tendency to be bitter. Most folks like their celery green, but pink- and red-stemmed varieties are available. Purple and red mustards like Osaka Purple have been popular for 10 years or more, and of course, there's always the red onion, red or speckled lettuce, radishes in every color of the rainbow, even red turnips, and kale. Designer vegetables are everywhere. Order some catalogs or go online—you'll be amazed.

Ethnic vegetables have hit it big-time, too. Many of the mainstay vegetables of Asian cuisine thrive in the cool season garden. Chinese cabbage and bok choy (pak choy, spoon cabbage) love our fall gardens. They have a tendency to bolt to seed in the spring garden but you may have overdosed on them by that time anyway. Chinese kale (gai lon), which looks like a small broccoli, mustards, mizuna (a parsleylike Japanese green), daikon (huge radish), and many other Asian vegetables are easy to grow in the fall garden.

Broccoli raab (a Portuguese favorite), celeriac (swollen celery root popular in Europe), celtuce with lettucelike leaves and tender, edible stems, corn salad (mache, a European salad green), various cresses from Upland to watercress, fennel, mesclun (a European mix of young salad greens), radicchio, rutabaga, parsnip, salsify, and scorzonera can all be grown in the southern kitchen garden.

VEGETABLE VARIETIES FOR THE SOUTHERN KITCHEN GARDEN

Check with the local Cooperative Extension Office for varieties specifically recommended for your area. Many of the following varieties will likely be included on the list. If local recommendations are not available, these varieties are a good place to start. You may also want to search the variety trials published in the websites of the various state Cooperative Extension agencies. It can be somewhat frustrating since the top producers are often commercial or wholesale varieties only available in large quantities to agricultural producers. If you run across a variety that you really want to try, do a web search and see if you can find a catalog supplier. If you have a bedding plant producer in your area, you

Sprouts

While you're at it, why not grow your own sprouts? Not only are they delicious, but they can be really, really good for your health—broccoli sprouts are an even better disease fighter (20–50 times the amount of sulforaphane) than the broccoli heads we usually consume. There are a variety of ways to produce sprouts. You can sprout seeds in a jar with a special lid, or use cheesecloth and a regular jar ring or rubber band. You can also find dozens of special sprouting trays that will get the job done. For most gardeners, it's best to start small. You can easily cover a kitchen counter with sprouts that the family won't eat or that they only want in small amounts. Start with a jar or two at first and maybe go with the sprouts that will add flavor and nutrition to a favorite stir-fry dish; then slip a few into salads or put a layer on the next sandwich.

The sprouting routine typically begins with a careful inspection of the seeds to remove damaged seeds or debris, and then you soak them overnight. In the morning you rinse and place the seeds in the sprouting container. Now you're off to a good start, but you can't take a break—the seeds need to be rinsed two to three times per day and kept in the dark for the first 2 to 3 days. When the seeds begin to sprout, move them into the light; after 3 to 6 days, you harvest them. Some of the seeds you can sprout include alfalfa, crucifers (broccoli, etc.), grass (barley, oats, rye, and wheat), peas, lentils, soybeans, and mung beans. There's a wealth of information on sprouting—both written and on the Internet. Each plant species has its own particular requirements, and it pays to investigate before you launch whole-hog into the sprouting game.

may also be able to get them to produce transplants of a promising tomato or other vegetables.

Asparagus	Jersey Giant Hybrid, Jersey Knight Hybrid, Purple Passion
Beans, bush	Contender, Jade, Topcrop, Provider, Derby, Maxibell, Roma II, Florence
Beans, pinto	Improved Pinto
Beans, pole	Kentucky Wonder, Dade, Purple King, Romano, Rattlesnake
Beans, lima	Bush-Jackson, Wonder, Henderson Bush, Fordhook 242, Pole-Florida Butter, Sieva (Carolina)
Beets	Chioggia, Detroit Red, Green Top Bunching, Pacemaker III
Broccoli	Bonanza, Emperor, Gypsy, Packman, Southern Comet, Early Dividend, Genji

Brussels sprouts	Diablo, Jade Cross, Tasty Nugget, and other hybrids
Cabbage	Early Jersey Wakefield, Savoy Hybrids, Golden Acre, Point One, Sombrero, Ruby Perfection (Red)
Carrots	Bolero, Danvers 126, Purple Haze, Scarlet Nantes
Cauliflower	Snow Crown Hybrid, Majestic, White Cloud, Graffiti (Purple), Violet Queen (purple), Cheddar (orange), Panther (green)
Chinese cabbage	Jade Pagoda, Tropical Delight, China Pride
Celery	Tango Hybrid, Utah, Florida, Cutting Celeries; Afina, Dinant
Chard, Swiss	Bright Lights, Rainbow, Rhubarb
Collards	Champion, Flash, Georgia, Green Glaze, Blue Max
Corn, sweet	Merit, Bonanza
Corn, sugar-enhanced	Funk's G-90, Kandy Korn, Tendertreat
Corn, supersweet	How Sweet It Is, Crisp 'n Sweet, Honey 'n Pearl, Summer Sweet, Florida Staysweet
Corn, triple-sweet	Honey Select, Serendipity
Corn, white	Silver Queen
Cucumbers, pickling	Calypso, Carolina, H-19 Little Leaf
Cucumber, slicers	Diva, Sweet Slice, Sweet Success, Garden Oasis, Suyo
Eggplant	Fairy Tale, Neon, Ping Tung Long, Raveena (green), Patio Mohican, Thai Long Green, Listada de Gandia
Garlic	Texas White, Mexican Purple (soft-neck varieties), Elephant

Kale	Red Russian, Redbor, Nero di Toscana, Dwarf Blue Curled
Kohlrabi	Grand Duke Hybrid, Express Forcer, Purple Danube, Kossak
Leek	Blue Solaise, Lancelot, Lincoln
Lettuce, leaf	Salad Bowl, Redina, Oakleaf, Green Ice, Red Sails, Red Fire, Vulcan
Lettuce, butterhead	Summer Bibb, Esmeralda, Buttercrunch
Lettuce, romaine	Valmaine, Little Caesar, Giant Caesar, Plato II
Melons, cantaloupes	Ambrosia, Luscious, Magnum 45 (cantaloupes), Honeymoon, Tam-Dew (honeydew), Amy Hybrid (canary), Lilly (Crenshaw), Savor (charentais)
Melons, watermelons	Watermelons Jubilee, Mickeylee, Crispy Critter, Pinata, Redlicious Seedless Var. Gem-Dandy, Lemon Ice Hyb., Sweetheart, Orange Sunshine
Mustard	Tender Green, Florida Broadleaf
Mustard, Chinese	Lei Chow, Purple Osaka, Giant Red Leaf
Okra	Clemson Spineless, Louisiana Green Velvet, Emerald, Perkin's Long Pod, Zeebest
Onions, plants/bulbing	Burgundy, Granex (white, yellow, and red), Texas SuperSweet
Onions, green	Ishikura, Summer Bunching, Evergreen White Bunching
Peas, southern	Mississippi Silver, Blackeye No. 5, Purple Hull, Queen Ann, Cream 40, Texas Pink Eye
Peas, English	Sugar Snap, Oregon Sugar Pod, Maestro
Peppers, sweet bell	Gypsy, Belltower, Big Bertha, Bell Captain, Jackpot, Lilac Hybrid, Golden Summer

Peppers, other	Banana Supreme, Laparie, Aji Dulce, Vera Cruz
Peppers, hot	Super Cayenne, Tabasco, Fresno Chile, Serrano Chile, Hungarian Wax, Jalapeño, Habanero
Potatoes, Irish/red	Red Lasoda, Red Pontiac, Rose Finn Apple (fingerling)
Potatoes, white	Kenebec, Yukon Gold, Russian Banana (fingerling)
Potatoes, russet	Norgold
Pumpkins	Howden, Big Moon, Baby Pam, Baby Bear AAS
Radish	Cherry Belle, Early Scarlet Globe, White Icicle, Champion
Radish, winter	Black Spanish, White Chinese, Daikon
Spinach	Early Hybrid 7, Melody, Tyee, Space, Baby Leaf, Reddy
Spinach, summer	New Zealand, Malabar
Squash, winter	Acorn, Butternut, Vegetable Spaghetti, Sweet Mama, Buttercup
Squash, summer	Dixie, Multipik, Hybrid Crookneck, White Bush Scallop, Sunburst, Zucchini Hybrids like Richgreen, Sundance, Tromboncino (a wild growing *C. moschata* species used like zucchini when green or like a winter squash if brown and mature)
Sweet potatoes	Centennial, Jewel, Beauregard
Tomatoes, large	Amelia, Dona, Carmello, Champion, Better Boy, Carnival, Terrific, Celebrity, 444 Hybrid, Bush Celebrity, First Lady
Tomatoes, small	Jolly, Juliette, Sweet 100 Hybrid, Chelsea, Enchantment (paste type with flavor and juice)
Turnips, roots/tops	Purple Top White Globe, White Lady, Tokyo Cross, Royal Globe
Turnips, greens	Seven Top, Shogoin

ETHNIC SPECIALTY GARDENS

Theme gardens can be fun and practical. If Mexican food is your passion, then group the vegetables, herbs, fruits, and flowers together in a garden that will inspire you to prepare these dishes at home. The warm season version of this garden could include jalapeño and serrano peppers, tomatillos, chayote squash, green beans, corn (if you have room), potatoes, and tomatoes combined with cilantro (early in the spring but it will bolt to seed in late spring), chives, oregano, Mexican oregano, Mexican marigold (a good tarragon substitute), and epazote. During the cool season plant onions, cilantro, and all of the more traditional vegetables like broccoli, lettuce, turnips, and spinach. Flowers in addition to the fall-flowering Mexican marigold could include regular marigolds, cosmos, zinnias, rainlilies, tigridia, and dahlias.

The Asian garden is better adapted to the cool season with Chinese cabbage, bok choy, mustard, radishes, mizuna, and a host of other leafy vegetables. Cilantro, chives, and bunching onions round out the fall garden—like both? Then do Mexican in the summer and Asian in the fall/winter. Asian crops for the summer include amaranth greens, basil (especially Holy or Thai varieties), adzuki beans, hyacinth bean, soybean, winged bean (love the scientific name—*Psophocarpus tetragonolobus*), yard-long bean, bitter melon, cucumber, eggplant, calabash gourd, hairy melon (also called fuzzy squash or melon), vining okra (luffa), Malabar spinach, Asian melons, hot peppers (Asian varieties like Yatsufusa), perilla, tomatoes (the Japanese like pink tomatoes—Odoriko is a good one), and Asian winter squash like Blue Kuri.

Other theme gardens might include an Indian garden with curry plants and patchouli or a Mediterranean garden—for example, the Italian pizza/pasta garden with basil, oregano, paste tomatoes, and a pepperoni plant. Sorry, the latter doesn't exist, but wouldn't it be cool if it did? The message here is to have fun with your garden.

THREE

herbs

While vegetables are the mainstay of the kitchen garden, herbs are almost as much of a necessity. Often good-quality vegetables are available at the farmer's market or even the grocery store, but the herbs you need for dilly mashed potatoes (only fresh dill will do) or cilantro for fresh salsa may be unavailable. Since a number of herbs are perennial, it is usually best to have separate beds for perennials and annuals. Even the perennials like rosemary and oregano will need to be renovated yearly with weeding and pruning. Another solution might be to have separate beds for warm season and cool season herbs. During the cool season, after the basil and other hot-weather-loving herbs die back, use the warm season bed to grow lettuce for the winter. In the warm season, plant a few hot peppers in the cool season herb bed to replace the parsley, dill, and fennel as they fizzle in the heat.

As you travel throughout the world, it is easy to see how local herbs have affected regional cuisines. What would Italian dishes be like without the addition of Mediterranean herbs like rosemary and oregano? Chiles and other hot peppers from the Americas add spice to local dishes throughout Mexico, Central and South America, the Caribbean, and they've found a home in Asian and Indian cuisine as well. Can you imagine salsa without a little cilantro?

Most herbs are easy to grow. With a little care and proper soil preparation, you, too, should be able to spice up your kitchen garden with these carefree and in many cases beautiful plants. When selecting a site, it's important to keep in mind that most culinary herbs prefer full sun and good air circulation.

Also, the majority of herb species need good drainage, so planting in raised beds is a natural. Even water-demanding herbs like mint will thrive in raised beds if you provide irrigation and plenty of fertilizer. Herbs are also a natural for pots or hanging baskets. This way you can keep them close to the back door and ready for the pan.

Sunlight is of the utmost in importance. In order for most herbs to develop the maximum amount of volatile oils, they must be grown in a bright, sunny location. Full sun is the best exposure, but if you can't plant your herbs where they will receive full sun most of the day, try to find a location that receives at least 6 to 8 hours of direct sunlight.

For best results, select a soil that is fertile, loamy, and well drained. Most herbs are very tolerant of soil type, but not drainage. A poorly drained soil that tends to hold moisture for long periods during rainy weather will ultimately lead to disaster. Planting in raised beds is an excellent way to improve drainage. Also, the addition of coarse builder's sand, cracked pea gravel, poultry grit, fine gravel, fired clay (calcined clay), haydite, or a similar material can be used to help break up tight, poorly drained soils. The soil pH (acidity or alkalinity) should range from 6.5 to 7.0. Many growers advocate the use of crushed limestone gravel in the soil. Limestone gravel may also be used as a mulch around many of the Mediterranean herbs such as rosemary, thyme, or lavender to improve drainage as well as to add needed calcium.

Organic matter is another important soil amendment. The addition of compost, leaf mold, or partially decomposed pine bark will help the soil to retain moisture, to remain friable (easy to work), and to hold nutrients. Don't be afraid to add generous amounts of organic matter to your garden each year, and incorporate it into the soil around your plants. Mulching with organic mulch is another way of building organic matter in the soil.

Many herbs are native to poor, rocky soils. As a result, they don't require an excessive amount of fertilizer in order to stay alive and reasonably healthy. They do seem to benefit from an occasional application of a good general fertilizer. Slow-release products such as cottonseed meal, encapsulated fertilizer, and many others, applied in the spring and late summer, are usually more than adequate to keep the plants healthy and happy. Overfertilization will tend to cause an excessive amount of green growth. This excessive growth is usually of poor culinary quality—low in the volatile oils that give herbs their fragrance and flavor.

Pests are relatively few, but the occasional spider mite may find your rosemary and grasshoppers love basil. Stick to organic pest controls and cultural techniques to ensure that you get your share of the herbs since you will be dealing with a mix of herbs at various stages of harvest.

Full sun is a requirement for the majority of herbs, but the leafy sorts will tolerate some shade, and mints thrive with some afternoon shade. A lot of herbs can be grown from seed, but many are propagated by cuttings too. In the case of long-lived herbs like rosemary, true bay, oregano, and scented geraniums there are even some named varieties from cuttings. Seed-grown herbs like basil, dill, and fennel are popular enough that a number of varieties have been developed of these herbs as well.

PERENNIAL HERBS

Chives, being a member of the onion family, really prefer the cool season, but it is surprising how long they will produce into the summer, and they usually recover with cooler weather in the fall. Include the flat-bladed or garlic chives and you have a true perennial—almost a weed. Both are easiest to start from seed in the fall, but they can also be divided or purchased as transplants in pots from the nursery. The baked potato you get at the restaurant "with chives" usually has chopped green onions on it—you'll be amazed how mulch milder and better tasting chives are. Go easy on the garlic chives—they may seem bitter if overused.

Mexican marigold is a true marigold (*Tagetes lucida*) that makes a good substitute for tarragon. It can be used for teas, in salads, or as a garnish with its pleasant root beer–like fragrance.

Mints come in a variety of flavors and fragrances. Some are well mannered, like peppermint and spearmint; others, like orange mint, can take over the garden. Try sinking a large unglazed ceramic pot in the herb bed with about 4 inches of the pot out of the soil. Plant the vigorous mints in this and keep the runners trimmed back, and even these mints shouldn't be a problem. While many herbs thrive in a gravelly soil, the mints appreciate a rich organic soil.

Oregano and its somewhat milder close relative sweet marjoram are perennial in most southern gardens. They may occasionally die out or need a good trimming to bring them back in shape, but they are quite reliable. Greek oregano is less cold hardy and usually has to be replanted in the spring. A number of unrelated plants also have the oregano oils such as Mexican oregano (*Poliomintha longiflora*) and *Lippia graveolens* (also referred to as Mexican oregano). These last two are somewhat shrubby and good candidates for the Mexican cuisine specialty garden.

The bay laurel or red bay develops into a large shrub or small tree. The true bay laurel is a Mediterranean shrub known for the bay leaf that often finds its way into our stews. It is marginally hardy north of the Gulf Coast, but you might want to try growing it in a large pot if fresh bay leaf is a frequently used item in your kitchen. Red bay makes a pretty good substitute (both are in the laurel family); it's a bit milder but hardier and easy to grow.

Lavender is one of the highly prized plants of the kitchen garden. Unfortunately, its silver foliage and beautiful lavender and pink flowers are a challenge to grow in the southern environment. The first step to success is to select varieties adapted to the more humid, moist climate of the southeastern United States. The next requirement is to prepare an extremely well-drained soil for the lavender plant to grow in; consider planting in 3 to 4 inches of gravel. Lastly, don't be disappointed if this short-lived perennial has to be replaced every 2 or 3 years. Some of the better types of lavender for the southern kitchen garden include Sweet lavender Goodwin Creek (*L. heterophylla*), French lavender (*L. dentate*), and Spanish lavender (*L. stoechas*).

Rosemary is another perennial herb that is more reliably hardy from the Gulf Coast South. There are prostrate forms that make good groundcovers and upright forms (Blue Lady) that can make a small to medium-sized shrub. This is an easy one to overdo in the kitchen, but used sparingly, it makes breads and Mediterranean dishes zing. Even a casual brush of the hand along this herb can suffice as

Oregano has a luxuriant trailing habit. As soon as it begins to invade other plants cut it back and dry the leaves for the freshest tasting, most wonderful oregano this side of the kitchen garden.

the southern kitchen garden

Lemongrass may look like the weed Johnson grass but it has the mildest, most refined lemon flavor you could ever imagine. Use it to prepare a soothing tea or to prepare lemongrass chicken.

a subtle perfume to start your day. Varieties such as Hills Hardy or Arp (both upright forms) and Blue Boy or Huntington (prostrate forms) are well suited for the southern garden.

Savory comes in a perennial form (winter savory) and an annual form (summer savory). Both do best in the cool season in our southern gardens, and even winter savory isn't always that long lived a perennial. The summer heat and moisture can weaken or take out both forms.

Thyme comes in many forms and flavors. There is common thyme, creeping thyme, lemon, caraway, and nutmeg thyme—and that's just a start. It's also available in variegated and woolly leaf forms. Thyme also suffers in the summer, but in raised beds with excellent drainage, it often survives to thrive again in the cool season.

Other perennial herbs include anise hyssop—a nice addition to the flower border that makes a good tea; catnip—pretty and the cats will love you; scented geraniums—hardy from the Gulf Coast South; lemon balm—a sprawling shrub with strong, lemon-flavored leaves; lemongrass with a wonderful, mild lemon taste and fragrance (though not too hardy); and sage—especially the narrow-leaved Israeli variety New'e Yare that is tolerant of heat and humidity.

Cilantro, also called coriander (especially for the seeds), is important to so many of the world's cuisines. Asian, Indian, and Hispanic cooks have led the way in the use of this rather strong herb. The French, at least in the nineteenth-century book *The Vegetable Garden* by Vilmorin, noted that "all the green parts of the plant exhale a very strong odor of the wood-bug"—a type of stinkbug. Maybe, but what would salsa be without it—spicy marinara sauce? And talk about exhaling. Have you tried some of the French goat cheeses?

COOL SEASON ANNUAL HERBS

Arugula may be a salad green to some folks, but it has a very strong flavor and needs to be grown sparingly and used more like a fresh herb for the majority of us. Comparing it with a dirty sock dipped in horseradish really isn't fair, but it is a difficult culinary experience to describe.

Cilantro is another strong-flavored herb. It takes some time to develop a taste for it, but once your taste buds lock on to cilantro, you're hooked. Fresh salsa just isn't good without it, and it adds zip to many sauces and soups. It is difficult to grow in the summer, but weekly sowings may suffice if you cut it often to prevent flower formation. Otherwise you will have to freeze some or buy it fresh from the store. Suppliers must ship it in from the high-altitude tropics during this season as it requires cool temperatures and short days to promote strong vegetative growth.

Dill can usually be planted in late winter for an early summer crop to go with your pickles, but it is much easier to grow in the fall and winter. In fact, they don't call it "dill weed" for nothing. It reseeds with a vengeance but is really quite easy to weed out or thin. Sometimes the tomato hornworms strip it to the stems, but they can be controlled if you catch them early.

the southern kitchen garden

Dill loves cool weather so it's best planted in the fall, but with a late planting in March or April you should be able to coax it along to mature with your cucumbers for dill pickles. Through the fall and winter snip some to mix with cheesy scrambled eggs—oh, and throw in some chives too. Next time you prepare homemade mashed potatoes add a cup of sour cream and a tablespoon or two of dill and chives, then top with real butter. These potatoes are so good you may forget to eat your chicken-fried steak.

Parsley thrives in cool weather; then it often dies in the heat of summer. This is especially true of the plain-leaved Italian types. They quickly bolt to seed in late spring and then die. The curly leaf varieties often persist well into the summer, so for most gardeners the choice is obvious. The curly leaf varieties also make a great border plant.

WARM SEASON ANNUAL HERBS

Basil is the dominant annual herb in the summer garden. It's available in a wide variety of forms and flavors, all of which flourish in the southern kitchen garden during the summer. It is not unusual to find 10 or more varieties listed in a seed catalog. For instance, there's a cinnamon-flavored basil or Lemon Sweet Dani (a 1998 All America selection). There are small-leaf varieties like Minette, or you can grow Large Leaf Italian. Purple Ruffles and Red Rubin can add color to the planting. If fusarium wilt has been a problem, plant Nufar Hybrid, the first wilt-resistant variety. This is a plant that is really sensitive to cold—it doesn't even like 40° temperatures. Heat, however, drives this plant to be extremely vigorous. You will need to prune it often to keep it from flowering and to keep it from taking over less aggressive perennial herbs. A new sweet basil that virtually never goes to seed is Summerlong. It produces an almost never-ending supply of large flavorful leaves.

    Epazote is a popular herb used in Mexican cuisine—especially in bean dishes. However, it, too, can become a weed, and a little goes a long way. Consider planting only one plant and don't let it go to seed.

MEXICAN HERBS

These versatile herbs delight garden guests, offering both ornamental and culinary virtue with their lively aromas, colors, textures, and flavors. Many are herbaceous shrubs that add form and texture to the garden and explode into a colorful array of flowers in the fall. The increasing popularity of these Mexican herbs makes them easily available at many local nurseries or by mail order.

Chile petin (pequin)	*Capsicum* spp.	Annual
Epazote, wormwood, goosefoot	*Chenopodium ambrosioides*	Annual
Chaya (medicinal)	*Cnidoscolus chaymansa*	
Cilantro, coriander	*Coriandrum sativum*	Cool season annual
Jamaica, tea hibiscus	*Hibiscus sabdariffa*	Tropical per. (Annual)
Mexican oregano	*Lippia graveolens*	Annual
Yerba buena	*Mentha spicata*	
Albacar (Mexican spice basil)	*Ocimum basilicum* Mexican Spice	Annual

Basil is one of the real herbal treats of the summer. Enjoy it in pesto, spaghetti, and sprinkle it on pizza. Cut it often to keep it from going to seed and you will have an abundant supply until fall temperatures begin to dip into the 40s.

Epazote is an important herb in Mexican cuisine—especially bean dishes. Be careful with this one, though, it can be a genuine weed. To be safe grow it in a pot or confine it to a small area of the herb bed with a section of 8-inch tile pipe.

Aztec sweet herb	*Phyla scaberrima (Lippia dulcis, Stevia rebaudiana)*	
Hoja santa, root beer plant	*Piper auritum*	
Mexican oregano	*Poliomintha longiflora*	Annual
Papaloquelite	*Porophyllum ruderale*	Annual
Pineapple sage	*Salvia elegans*	
Mexican bush sage (ornamental)	*Salvia leucantha*	

Copper Canyon daisy (ornamental)	*Tagetes lemmonii*	Annual
Yerbanis, Mexican mint marigold	*Tagetes lucida*	Annual

TRIMMING HERBS

Like most plants, herbs benefit from an occasional trimming or shearing. In fact, if you harvest regularly, additional trimming or pruning won't be required. By cutting back your herbs during the process of harvesting or as routine mainte-nance, you accomplish a number of beneficial things. Cutting back herbs during the summertime can make them much more attractive and neater, adding to the aesthetic value of your kitchen garden. Cutting back also stimulates new growth, and new growth is needed to produce quality herbs for the kitchen. Cutting back can also be used as a way of removing flowers and spent seed pods. Many herbs such as mint, basil, oregano, and others have to be pruned to discourage flowering so that the plants spend more of their energy in the development of the desired foliage. A lot of gardeners are reluctant to prune their herbs for fear that it will damage or hurt them, but nothing could be further from the truth. Most herbs benefit greatly from the occasional haircut. Don't be afraid to grab the utility scis-sors and head out to the herb garden to tidy up.

the fruit garden

Fruit production may seem too complicated or space demanding for most kitchen gardeners, but we can usually find room for a few berry plants, or the specimen trees in the landscape can be peaches or plums instead of ornamentals. Citrus is a good choice for kitchen gardeners from the Gulf Coast South. And if you don't mind moving a few pots into the greenhouse, a container-grown Mexican lime, Meyer lemon, or Satsuma is possible for the entire South.

The main consideration is, What fruits do you really crave that are best harvested fresh from the tree or vine? Of course, it has to be something that will grow well, too, or you'll be butting your head against a wall. This pretty much rules out raspberries, gooseberries, and the like. If you're in an area with alkaline soil, then you can forget blueberries without building extreme raised beds.

Maybe the most perplexing decisions to deal with involve variety selection. We've tried to profile some of the most reliable varieties for the kitchen garden, but the variety availability is constantly changing. Start with recommendations from this book and your local Cooperative Extension Center, referred to as the County Agent's Office in most areas of the South. Search the Internet if you can, and then check with local nurseries, mail-order nurseries, and local fruit grower groups. If certain varieties keep coming up with high recommendations, then you are beginning to narrow down your selections. Fruit production is typically an 8- to 10-year investment in your time, so it pays to get it right before you plant.

It is also important to consider the chill requirements of the trees you are selecting. Most temperate climate plants (fruit trees are no exception) require a certain amount of chilling each winter in order for flowering and vegetative buds to develop properly. A number of different chill models are being used today. The one most commonly used in the South describes chilling as the accumulation of hours of temperatures in the range between 32°F to 45°F. The number of hours accumulated each winter can range from anywhere between 100 hours along the Gulf Coast to as much as 800 to 1,000 hours in the northern part of the southeastern

65

United States. It's important to select varieties that require, plus or minus approximately 100 hours, what you normally receive in your area. You should be able to obtain the average chill hours for your area from your local County Extension Office or the National Weather Service.

You can topwork (regraft or rebud) most fruit and nut trees if they haven't grown too large, but it requires some skill and a lot of aftercare to change varieties after the fact. Of course, there are always the passionate enthusiasts who must have every variety known to man, and they end up with "fruit salad" trees with multiple varieties grafted on each tree. Generally you will have to stick to one species per tree, but closely related species like plum, peach, nectarine, and apricot will usually survive on the same tree. The new hybrids like pluot and aprium are also compatible. Apples and pears are close but often develop incompatibilities, and the graft eventually fails. If you must have a fruit salad tree, it is safest to stay with the stone fruits. As long as you stay within the genus, though, you can graft away. For example, you can have multiple apple varieties on one apple tree, multiple pear varieties on one pear, pecans, and so forth.

SMALL SPECIMEN TREES

Whether you can justify a miniorchard or not, you still need to consider the special requirements for good fruit production. Even one or two trees need good soil, full sun, air drainage—you don't want to plant in a low area of the landscape sometimes referred to as a frost pocket—cross-pollination (if necessary), and, of course, you must plant adapted varieties. Planting dwarf trees is one answer to the space problem, but not all dwarfing rootstocks are adapted to the South. Genetic dwarfs—especially peaches and nectarines—show promise, but there are a limited number of varieties adapted to our relatively low-chill weather conditions. Training systems and pruning can often save the day by directing the growth of fruit trees into a single plane as an espalier against a wall, and the mere act of pruning is a dwarfing process.

PRUNING, TRIMMING, AND TRAINING

Gardeners prune plants for a variety of reasons ranging from such things as increasing flowering or fruiting and promoting stronger more productive growth to removing diseased or damaged tissue and even for reasons as arbitrary as "everyone else is doing it." One of the first things to think about when considering pruning, trimming, or training is whether or not there's a good reason for doing it. If you can't come up with one, then put the clippers away.

It will be necessary to prune and train a number of plants commonly found in the kitchen garden. Trimming is used extensively when harvesting herbs as well as maintaining size and appearance of flowering and fruiting plants.

Fruit trees comprise the major group of plants that require routine pruning and training. The two primary reasons for pruning and training fruit trees are to establish a basic structure and to encourage the admission of light throughout the canopy of the tree so that all the fruit can mature with good color. A well-pruned tree is easier to maintain and to harvest and can add to the aesthetic value of the tree as well. Have you ever noticed that the best fruit always seems to be in the top of the tree? You've probably thought that's because they're out of reach, but the primary reason is that these are the fruits that receive the most light.

Three tools will be required to handle most of the common pruning and training jobs. You'll find that most pruning and training can be accomplished with a good pair of scissor-style hand pruners, a pair of long-handled lopping shears, and a sharp pruning saw. Many first-time gardeners try to skimp by purchasing cheap pruning equipment. A word to the wise, you generally get what you pay for. By purchasing high-quality equipment, you'll find that your pruning and training chores will be much more enjoyable and require less effort. A good pair of utility or florist shears is great for trimming back herbs or cutting flowers for the kitchen.

PRUNING AND TRAINING FRUIT TREES

All major pruning should be done during the normal dormant season. This occurs sometime in the late fall after all growth has ceased. It is also best to finish pruning before the activation of growth in the spring. It's best not to delay pruning chores until the last minute because conditions may vary during any given year and mild temperatures could initiate spring growth before you can finish the job. Some gardening books will recommend summer pruning. This is a common practice in dry climates where disease is much less of an issue. In the southeastern United States, where rainfall can be abundant and humidity will usually run high, it's best to avoid summer pruning whenever possible. It also should be noted that proper sanitation should be exercised in order to reduce the spread of disease. Taking a few moments after pruning a tree to disinfect your pruning equipment with either isopropyl alcohol or a mild chlorine solution (one part chlorine bleach to nine parts water) can make a big difference in the overall health of your trees.

There are two major types of pruning cuts commonly made when pruning fruit trees: thinning and heading. *Thinning* is the removal of an entire shoot, branch, or limb back to the point where it originated. Thinning cuts are used because they open up the canopy allowing light to penetrate into the tree. Often just thinning out the limbs that are crowding or crossing does not do enough to effectively open up the tree. *Heading* is removing part of a shoot, branch, or limb (up to one-third–two-thirds of its length). Heading cuts encourage the development of side branches at the point of the cut and are used primarily for establishing branches in young trees. Leaders or future scaffold branches can be headed back to encourage laterals to branch out. Heading should be used sparingly because it can result in a tree that is overcrowded with shoots, reducing productivity. When heading is necessary, such as to shorten and stiffen up a long bare branch, make the heading cut into older wood, because it will result in less regrowth.

Two major training systems are commonly used for tree fruits. The group of plants referred to as stone fruits (peaches, nectarines, plums, apricots, sour cherries, and almonds) are trained using a technique called *open center*. The other major training system typically used on pome fruits (apples, mayhaws, quince, crab apple, and pear), persimmons, and pecans is referred to as the central leader or modified central leader pruning system.

No tree exactly fits any one training system. Pruning a tree means being aware of how light affects growth and how its structure develops over time. The art of pruning is developing balanced growth that is productive and aesthetically pleasing. Don't worry about making mistakes. It takes time to develop the skills needed to properly prune your fruit trees. The best way to learn is by doing, and the trees are very forgiving. Pruning and training are an important part of proper fruit tree care, so grab your pruning equipment and jump in with both feet. Most people don't prune out enough of the fruiting wood rather than pruning out too much. If you make mistakes one year, you may be able to correct your mistakes with heavier pruning in future years.

Open Center Training System

The open center training system has been used extensively throughout the United States. When properly executed, it creates a vase-shaped tree that can easily be sprayed, pruned, and harvested from the ground. Peaches, nectarines, almonds, and, to a lesser extent, plums, apricots, and sour cherries bear fruit on last season's growth. The open center training system creates a structure that allows sunlight to reach the interior of the tree, encouraging the development of fruiting branches on the lower scaffold limbs. By developing new branches lower on the tree, we can encourage continued production over a long period of time. As was mentioned earlier, light is also important in the development and ripening of fruit. Regular pruning is required to encourage the development of new growth. Without proper pruning, this group of fruits will reduce growth to the point that little fruiting wood is produced. Once this occurs, production ceases.

It's important to start the training process early. It should begin the day the tree is planted. When selecting one of the above-mentioned fruit trees, find a vigorous, healthy 4- to 6-foot-tall tree. There is no major advantage to starting with extremely large trees. Transplant shock can be significant, and a large tree is much more difficult to start training.

- **Year 1**. When the tree is planted, it should be cut back to somewhere between 24 and 42 inches. We are trying to encourage the formation of scaffold branches fairly low on the tree. Most commercial orchards will prune back to approximately 24 inches. Some gardeners prefer a tree that is a little taller, with scaffold branches well above the ground for aesthetic reasons and to facilitate mowing and other gardening activities. Remember that the higher you start the first scaffold branches the taller the tree will ultimately be and therefore the more difficult it will be to properly spray, harvest, and maintain. All side branches should be removed at this time as well. This is a very difficult thing for gardeners to do. Who wants to look at a bare stick when you left the nursery with a branched tree? Be assured, however, that the new branches that arise from the trunk will be much stronger.

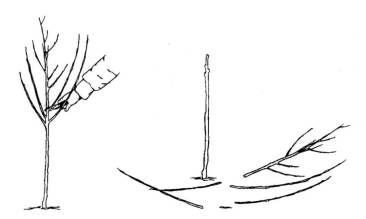

- **Year 2**. Once the tree has gone dormant, you can begin pruning and training. The second-year pruning is relatively simple. First, you should remove all water sprouts and suckers that have developed from the lower portion of the trunk. Next try to select three major scaffold branches near the top of the main trunk. These three scaffold branches should be evenly spaced in a tripod fashion. They should arise from the trunk of the tree at approximately a 45° to 65° angle. Try not to select a scaffold branch that is too horizontal or one that is too vertical. A branch angle of approximately 45° to 65° will add strength to the tree and promote desirable fruiting wood. It's not uncommon for the three remaining scaffold branches to have secondary branches. Remove any secondary branches that grow into the center of the tree or cross one another. The three major scaffold branches that you have selected will become a permanent part of the tree, and many of those secondary branches will remain for several years.

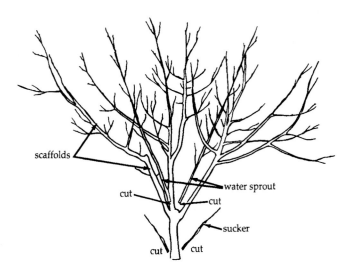

- **Year 3 and beyond**. Again, you'll want to wait until the tree has gone into dormancy (usually November through February). Pruning is a difficult task for many people, thus it's best to develop a training strategy that eliminates much of the guesswork. Generally this group of trees will begin bearing fruit sometime after their third year. Pruning from this point forward is important in the continued production of the tree. The first step is to remove all growth below the 3-foot line. That means all the water sprouts, suckers, and low-hanging branches are removed. The only thing remaining below the 3-foot line is the main trunk and permanent scaffold branches. The next step will be to cut the tree back to a workable height. This will vary depending on your particular needs to somewhere between 8 and 15 feet. A taller tree will generally produce more total pounds of fruit, but because of the increased height, it may be more difficult to spray, harvest, and prune. You'll have to decide which is best for your needs. Once the tree has been pruned back to the desired height, begin to remove and thin the interior branches. First select those branches that have grown across the center of the tree. It's important to open up the center of the tree, creating an open structure that allows sunlight penetration to the major scaffolds. Finally, you'll want to go in and selectively remove overcrowded branches as well as any diseased or broken limbs. You know you have removed enough of the canopy of the tree when approximately a third to half of the branches of the tree have been removed. Early-producing varieties should be pruned harder then later varieties.

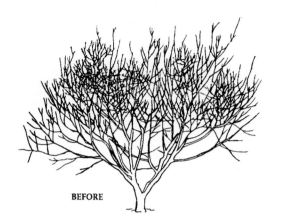

BEFORE

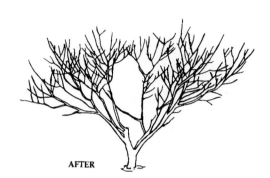

AFTER

Central Leader Training System

The central leader is well adapted to trees that have a naturally upright growth habit, which includes apple, pear, pecan, persimmon, and quince. It is quite often used on trees that have been grafted onto dwarf rootstock.

- **Year 1**. When the tree is planted, the main trunk or central leader should be lightly headed back, approximately one-third its length. If the tree has already developed side branches before planting, those side branches can be retained but should be lightly tipped back (remove approximately 3 inches); tipping is used to encourage the development of additional branches. Side branches should be selected to form the lowest or main scaffold, and trained outward at a 45° angle. Side branches that are more upright than 45° can be spread using limbs spreaders or weights to pull the branches down. Any branches that compete with the main trunk or central leader should be thinned out. Allow the tree to grow, selecting additional branches as they develop, and use limbs spreaders to force them out at approximate 45° angles from the trunk. If any branches begin to compete with the main trunk or central leader, they should be tipped back to slow growth or thinned out completely. Light pruning and training can be done during the growing season on this group of fruit trees.

the fruit garden

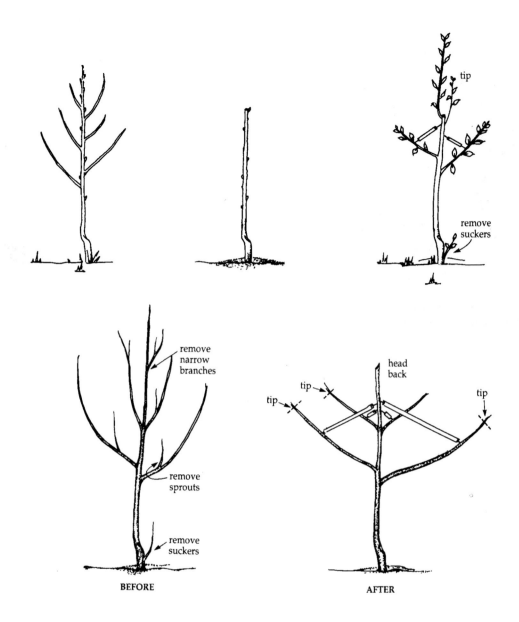

BEFORE

remove
narrow
branches

remove
sprouts

remove
suckers

tip

remove
suckers

head
back

tip

tip

tip

AFTER

■ **Year 2.** Once the tree has gone dormant, the main trunk or central leader should be lightly headed back about one-third its length, and the side branches should be tipped to encourage branching. Any very strong, upright growing limbs (water sprouts) should be removed at this time. Suckers off the main trunk or near the base of the tree should also be removed. During the second growing season, you should continue to select regularly spaced side branches, train those side branches outward at 45° angles, and remove any upright branches that are competing with the main trunk or central leader.

the southern kitchen garden

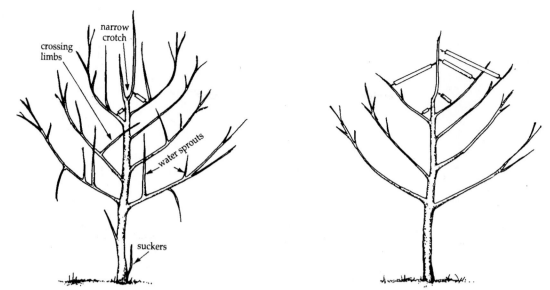

crossing
limbs

narrow
crotch

water sprouts

suckers

Remove sucker and water sprouts (vigorous upright shoots)

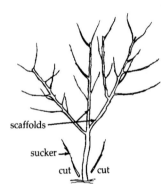

scaffolds

sucker

cut   cut

- **Year 3 and beyond**. Continue training the tree over the next 3 to 5 years, selecting scaffold branches that are evenly spaced along the main trunk of the tree. Encourage the branching structure to develop wide angles by using spacers to train the scaffolds to about 45° to 60° from vertical. Your goal should be to develop a tree with a profile that is something like a simplified Christmas tree. It should have a conical shape that is wide at the bottom and narrow at the top. Thin out the vigorous, upright shoots (water sprouts), and retain those that are less vigorous. Never allow the upper scaffolds to overgrow and shade the lower ones. Try to maintain about 60% of the tree's total volume in the lower scaffold brunches. This provides good access to light throughout the tree and makes it easier to care for the tree and to harvest the fruit.

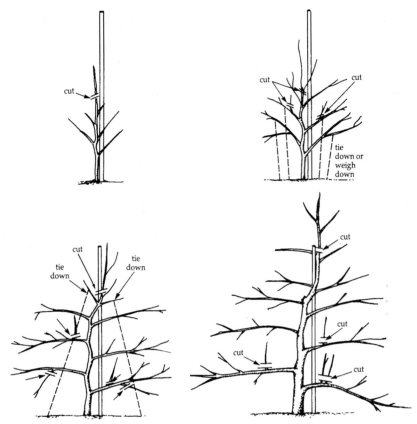

Training apple trees to a slender spindle system.

Blackberries and Raspberries (the Brambles)

Blackberries and raspberries, although not difficult to prune, definitely require a different approach. Blackberries and most raspberries produce their fruit on the previous season's growth.

The new shoots that are developing throughout the growing season (primocanes) become the fruiting canes (floricanes) during their second season of growth. Once the fruiting canes have finished producing, they are removed to allow the primocanes to grow and develop.

- Each year after the fruit is harvested, the old fruiting canes will need to be cut completely down to the ground. These old canes have done their job and will not produce again. Failure to remove the old fruiting canes will make the bramble difficult to manage and can contribute to increased disease and insect problems within the blackberry or raspberry planting.
- In the spring, the new primocanes will begin growing. Once they reach a height of approximately 36 to 42 inches, the tips of these canes should be removed. This tipping will help with the development of side branches,

the southern kitchen garden

which will develop additional fruit, thus increasing the total production of your planting. Failure to tip back the new canes will result in the development of very long, sprawling growth that becomes difficult to control.

■ Each year you will continue with this process of removing the old fruiting canes and tipping back the new developing shoots. By doing this, your planting should remain manageable, making it easier to pick and easier to prune in the future.

■ Some of the raspberry varieties are strictly fall bearing in the southern kitchen garden. These fall-bearing varieties are very easy to manage. Each winter when the plants have gone dormant, they should be cut back completely to the ground. The new canes that arise in the spring will terminate with flowers in the late summer and early fall. You should continue to prune these varieties back completely to the ground each year.

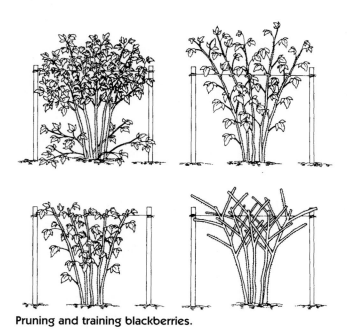

Pruning and training blackberries.

Grapes (Bunch and Muscadine)

A number of common training systems are used on grapes. Some are very simple while others can be quite complex. The following is a system of training that can be adapted to bunch grapes as well as muscadines. The cordon system of training requires the scaffold branches be supported by a wire or other structure. The fruiting canes develop off the scaffolds, and they are tied to some type of support as they develop. The system can easily be adapted to a variety of trellis structures or an arbor. This versatility makes it the perfect system for the kitchen garden.

- The grape plant is usually planted during the dormant season although container-grown plants extend the planting season for home gardeners. Drive a stake into the ground beside the vine, and use the stake to support the developing plant as it grows. Remove all the side branches on the newly planted vine and cut the vine back to two healthy buds.

- When new growth appears in the spring, select the strongest growing shoot and train it to the stake. Any other shoots that develop should be tipped back to suppress their development. Continue tipping back the side shoots to force as much of the plant's energy into the development of what will become the new trunk of your grapevine. This main shoot should be trained on the vertical support until it reaches the desired height. This will vary depending on the type of support you have built for your vineyard. With the cordon system of training, a number of different configurations can be used to support the vine. All of them have a horizontal support member that is used to support the permanent scaffolds of the vine.

- If the vine makes enough growth during the first growing season to reach the horizontal wire or support, the vine should be tipped back, and two side branches should be trained down the horizontal support in opposite directions.

- Once the vine has gone dormant, remove any side shoots that have developed on the main trunk, and tie the scaffold branches to the horizontal support wire.

- When new growth appears in the spring, continue training the horizontal scaffold branches until they reach the desired length. Generally bunch grapes are trained with scaffold branches that are approximately 4 feet long, making the total width of the grapevine 8 feet. The scaffold branches of muscadine grapes should be allowed to reach approximately 8 feet, making the total width of the grapevine 16 feet because muscadine grapes are much more vigorous, resulting in a larger plant. Once the desired length is reached, tip the scaffold branches back to encourage the development of side shoots.

- These side shoots will become the semipermanent fruiting spurs. The side shoots should be spaced out approximately 6 to 8 inches apart along the whole length of the scaffold branches.

- During the dormant season (this should be about year 3), each of the side shoots should be pruned back to two buds. This short shoot is called a fruiting spur. These fruiting spurs will continue to be cut back to two buds each year for the next several years on bunch grapes while the fruiting spurs will be maintained for a number of years on muscadine grapes.

- Each year during the dormant season you should remove all shoots that develop along the main trunk, keeping it completely clean, while cutting back all the shoots that have developed along the scaffold branches. Select your most vigorous side shoots, and prune them back to two new buds, forming next year's fruiting spurs. Every few years you should remove a few of the old fruiting spurs and select a few evenly spaced new shoots to train into new fruiting spurs. This is referred to as renewal pruning.

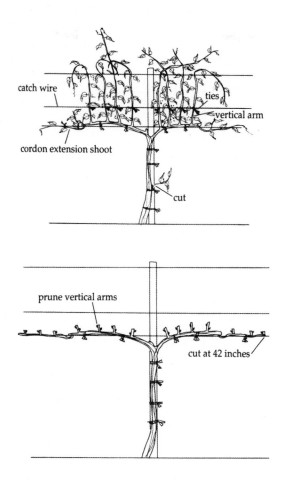

- Muscadines are handled a bit differently because of their inherent vigor. The fruiting spurs become more permanent features on the scaffold branches of muscadine grapes. The first year prune back the side shoots to two buds. These two buds grow to form two shoots that are then cut back to two buds each. You now have two short fruiting spurs. The next year these two fruiting spurs develop four shoots. These four shoots are then cut back to two buds resulting in the development of four fruiting spurs. The process continues for up to 8 or 10 years, developing a large mass of fruiting spurs originating from a single location along the scaffold branches. These clusters of fruiting spurs are referred to as hands. When these hands decline in vigor they should be completely removed and a new side shoot that is developing nearby should be selected, and the process starts all over again.

FRUIT VARIETY RECOMMENDATIONS

One of the biggest challenges in gardening is selection of the best and tastiest varieties to grow. There are several ways you can come up with this information. One is by trial and error. Just keep planting and tasting until you find varieties that grow well in your area and that taste good. This may be the best way to find the varieties you like, but with fruit and nut crops, you could spend a long time in research. Usually we shorten the process by checking out websites and recommended lists from our State Extension Service, or you may rely on friend's recommendations, the advice of a trusted nursery employee, or a good book. Be sure to check our resource list—it also includes fruit interest groups like the Southern Fruit Fellowship, California Rare Fruit Growers, and North American Fruit Explorers. These folks are extreme when it comes to fruit. We would like to assure you that every fruit tree or bush that you find at the local nursery or even the cash-and-carry nurseries will be true to label and adapted to your area but if we did you would soon know better and then you would doubt our credibility. We do think that locally owned nurseries probably try the hardest to sell the best-adapted varieties, but sometimes you have to mail order some variety because it's new or hard to find. Cash-and-carry nurseries are the least likely to know what's adapted to your area, and the plants may not be properly labeled. Often the garden center manager in these stores has little input into which varieties are available. It pays to study the grafting and budding section in this book if you buy from cheap and unreliable sources since you will likely need to graft adapted varieties on the bargain plants at a later date. Don't be discouraged if it's hard to find the varieties you want to try, especially if you find that the rootstocks we've mentioned are hard to come by. Get connected with fruit enthusiast groups, order your own rootstocks, and t-bud them to the latest varieties (provided they aren't patented)—you could end up with six to eight varieties on one tree. Before you know it, you'll have a tasty collection of fruit growing in a relatively small area. If the varieties you're after are patented, then you'll have to rely on a nurseryman licensed to propagate them and purchase them as single-variety trees.

Apples

Apples are one of the more demanding fruits to grow. They tolerate a wide range of soil types but require excellent drainage. Most of the southern apple varieties ripen in July or August, which lessens color development and reduces overall quality. There are several serious disease problems that require routine applications of a fungicide throughout the production season. In the Gulf Coast, this fruit is not recommended for those individuals interested in growing organically. Whenever possible, try to select varieties grafted on dwarf or semidwarf rootstock. Dwarf or espaliered apple trees make a lot of sense for gardeners in the upper South, but the number of varieties adapted to kitchen gardening from the Gulf Coast South is limited. Anna and Dorsett Golden (both are Golden Delicious seedlings) offer the most promise. They also bloom about the same time, so there is potential for good cross-pollination, which apples need for good fruit set. The challenge comes in finding a good dwarfing rootstock. EMLA 9 (30% of full size) is OK, but it definitely needs to be supported with stakes or a trellis as it simply can't support a fruit load on its limited root system. A step up in size (about 50% of a full-size tree) is EMLA 7. Both rootstocks are adapted to heavy soils but susceptible to bacterial fire blight. Trellising or staking lends itself well to the kitchen garden model, so all that remains is to find suitable varieties on the right rootstock. If you're interested in grafting or budding, you could buy a Dorsett Golden tree and graft a few branches of Anna into it—or vice versa. Apple rootstocks are rarely specified at the retail nursery level, but the enthusiast may be able to procure newer rootstocks like Ottawa-3 or Geneva 41 with a bit of Internet searching. Even then, rootstocks will usually have to be ordered 100 or more at a time, so be prepared to share with friends. The EMLA 7 rootstock (50% size and tolerant of clay soil) and EMLA 9 (30%, requires support) are more readily available—at least from mail-order sources.

APPLE VARIETIES

Apple Varieties	Chill Requirement (hours)	Ripe/Color	Remarks/Description
Akane	800	August. Red.	An excellent, red dessert apple derived from Jonathan with sweet, rich, spicy flavor. Resists scab and powdery mildew. Upper South variety.
Anna	100–300	Early July. Yellow-red blush.	Developed from Yellow Delicious. Quality is good within a narrow harvest window of 2–3 weeks. When picked too early, the fruit is sour and lacks flavor; picked too late, its texture is mealy. Anna is a self-fruitful variety.
Beverly Hills	400	July/August. Red/Yellow stripe.	Small, crisp apple with good flavor. Not self-fertile, so it has disappeared from the nursery scene because homeowners likely had little or no production. If planted with other low-chill varieties, like Anna or Dorsett Golden, to provide pollen this shouldn't be a problem.
Braeburn	700	August to September. Green with dark red blush.	New Zealand variety, very crisp and tangy, more flavorful than Granny Smith. Excellent keeper. Self-fruitful. Upper South only.
Dorsett Golden	100–200	Early July. Yellow.	Like Anna, it is at its prime for only a few weeks. Slightly sweeter than Anna, it is about the only variety that will bloom at the same time as Anna. Either variety will produce some fruit without cross-pollination, but production will be

(continued)

the fruit garden

79

Apple Varieties	Chill Requirement (hours)	Ripe/Color	Remarks/Description
			increased if both varieties are planted together. Einsheimer is another variety often listed with Anna and Dorsett; however, the quality is poor.
Fuji	400–600	Early August. Yellow-green, red stripes.	In spite of its poor appearance, this is one of the finest-quality apples in the world. The tree requires detailed pruning. Most people find it is a poor producer in the lower South. The variety Beni Shogun Fuji has a lower chill requirement and ripens earlier.
Gala	550–600	July–August. Red with yellow stripes.	Mostly an upper South variety, but it may also be worth a try along the upper Gulf Coast. Very high-quality fruit.
Golden Delicious	700	August–September. Golden.	Longtime favorite for its sweetness and flavor. Reliable producer, adapted to many climates. Pollinator for Red Delicious. Self-fruitful.
Granny Smith	600–800	Early August. Waxy green.	Good quality, tart, sweet fruit. Late maturity makes disease control difficult. This variety tends to be a light producer in the lower South.
Hudson's Golden Gem	550	Late July–August. Yellow-brown russeted fruit.	Chance seedling from Corvallis, Oregon. Good flavor—similar to a crunchy pear.
Pink Lady	600–650	Early August. Pink-red with yellow base color.	Very vigorous and upright, large wavy-edged leaves. Susceptible to scab and fire blight, fairly susceptible to powdery mildew. Firm, dense, fine flesh, crisp and juicy, excellent flavor.

Asian Pears

Asian pears are an excellent fruit for the South. They're very well adapted to the southern environment as long as the varieties selected have good resistance to bacterial fire blight. Assuming you've planted disease-resistant varieties, this is an excellent fruit for the organic gardener. It is important to plant more than one variety in order to get good cross-pollination and fruit set. Asian pear trees can get large, so be sure to provide them with plenty of space. Pear trees are adapted to a wide range of soil types as long as the drainage is adequate. Try to avoid wet spots or low-lying areas. Trees will generally take 5 to 7 years to come into production. Most of these pears have a round "apple shape," but some have the standard pyriform or hourglass shape.

Variety	Chill Requirement (hours)	Ripe/Color	Remarks/Description
20th Century or Nijisseiki	800–1,000	Mid-September. Green to greenish yellow.	Best-known Asian pear. Fruit is smooth with some lenticels (small bumps on the skin). Flesh is white, firm, crisp, very juicy, and sweet with a refreshing tartness. Fruit quality is good to very good. Upper South variety.
Hosui	400–500	August. Brownish-orange with russet.	Crisp with more flavor compared to other Asian varieties. Has shown considerable blight in recent years but still produces crops. Whether this variety can live with the disease like some others (e.g., Kieffer) remains to be seen. A chance seedling of Tenn with Hosui as a possible parent has been named Tennosui. The authors planted this tree from Tenn seed in the 1990s, and it is early (July/August), crisp (great fresh from the refrigerator), and the flesh is very slow to oxidize or turn brown. It may be a few years before this variety is readily available.
Kikusui	500	August. Greenish-yellow.	This variety doesn't store well, but the fruit is crisp, sweet, and juicy. Rather susceptible to bacterial fire blight.
Kosui	500–600	Late July–August. Yellow russetted.	Small fruit with very sweet taste. Susceptible to bacterial fire blight.
Shinko	600–800	Mid-October. Brown to golden brown russet.	Fruit is medium to large (14–20 oz.) with a yellowish white flesh with a good juicy, sweet flavor. Fruit quality is very good to excellent, and tree is very resistant to fire blight. Upper South variety.
Shinseiki	600–800	August. Yellow-green.	Medium-size fruit with a very mild flavor. The fruit hangs on the tree in good condition and stores as well. Very large and vigorous tree with healthy foliage. Upper South variety.
Ya Li, Shin Li, and Tsu Li	500–600	July–August. Yellow-green to slightly russeted and pyriform to semipyriform in shape.	These pyriform variations of the Asian pear are well adapted to the southern climate. It remains to be seen if they can survive the pressure of bacterial fire blight. Typically they are less susceptible to fungal leaf spot, but in dry years, they may be damaged almost as severely by spider mites.

Berries

Berry crops, especially blackberries, may be the most adapted of the fruit crops simply because of their smaller size. Granted, some crops like blackberries can be invasive because they spread rapidly, but they can be contained by digging out the extras, or you can contain them with a root barrier. Regardless, your best bet is to plant them in a separate bed so you can manage them without the worry of damaging other plants that may be growing in the bed when you need to dig up some of the old plants.

Blackberries are very well adapted to South. In fact, they are an excellent choice for organic gardeners because they have relatively few insect and disease problems. Also, since they are self-fruitful, you don't have to plant several varieties for cross-pollination. Generally the most productive blackberries are the upright varieties, which don't require a trellis or other means of support. The kitchen garden concept really cries out for the use of vertical space both for efficiency and to define spaces, so you may find a trellis not only makes it easier to keep your blackberries tidy but also just looks good in the garden. Most blackberries produce on new wood and require that the old fruiting canes be removed each year after harvest. It is also important to top the new primocanes (vigorous shoots but no flowers) at about 4 feet to encourage branching and more fruiting wood for next year's crop.

BLACKBERRY VARIETIES

Variety	Thorned/Thornless	Remarks/Description
Apache	Thornless	An excellent, relatively new release from University of Arkansas. The fruit is firm and sweet and ripens later than Arapaho. Apache is more productive and better adapted to the upper South than Arapaho. Plants appear to be resistant to rosette disease and orange rust.
Arapaho	Thornless	Arapaho is a strong upright-growing variety producing high-quality berries. Navaho and Arapaho were both released the same year but Arapaho appears to be better for the lower South. It appears to be resistant to orange rust and rosette diseases.
Brazos	Thorned	Brazos is an old variety released by Texas A&M University. It is very productive, producing large berries with large seed. The fruit is quite tart unless harvested when fully ripe.
Cheyenne	Thorned	Vigorous, erect, mid-season variety for the upper South. Cheyenne is an excellent-quality berry. Fruit is sweet, large, and has a slight raspberry flavor.
Chickasaw	Thorned	Another excellent, relatively new release from University of Arkansas. The fruit is very large, firm, and sweet. Better adapted to the upper South. Susceptible to rosette.
Kiowa	Thorned	Kiowa is one of the most recent releases from University of Arkansas. The berries are extremely large and sweet. The golfball-size fruit has small seed, good quality, and the bush is very productive. It is susceptible to rosette disease.

Variety	Thorned/Thornless	Remarks/Description
Navaho	Thornless	Navaho is an erect blackberry with medium-size fruit, high sugar, and excellent flavor. Navaho is tolerant of rosette but susceptible to orange rust.
Ouachita	Thornless	Ouachita is an erect thornless blackberry—a 2003 release from the University of Arkansas. The fruit is large with good quality. Fruit ripens with Kiowa and extends for about 5 weeks. Ouachita is resistant to rosette disease. Ouachita chill-hour requirements are probably similar to Arapaho.
Prime Jim and Prime Jane	Thorned	Prime Jim and Prime Jane are a new class of blackberries called primocane blackberries that produce fruit on current season canes as well as second-year canes. This production differs from standard blackberries that produce fruit only on 2-year-old canes. The University of Arkansas released these two primocane varieties in 2004. These varieties have produced good yields on primocanes in Oregon, but yields on primocanes have been very low in the Southeast. Temperatures exceeding 85°F tend to severely reduce fruit set, size, and quality on primocanes. Fruit on floricanes of these varieties has been similar to fruit yield on floricanes of Apache and Ouachita.
Rosborough	Thorned	Rosborough is an improved variety of Brazos developed by Texas A&M University. It is vigorous and upright, producing a heavy crop of sweet, small-seeded fruit. Rosborough is very susceptible to rosette disease.
Shawnee	Thorned	This is an excellent-quality, large berry on a very productive bush. The plant is upright and vigorous and best adapted to the upper South. Shawnee is very susceptible to rosette disease.
Womack	Thorned	Womack is another Texas A&M University release, similar to Rosborough, but it has smaller berries.

Blueberries are very demanding when it comes to soil and cultural requirements. Mostly they are finicky about soil; if the soil is right, they almost grow like weeds. Blueberries are a cinch in the South if you have a sandy, acid soil. While you can build raised beds filled with peat moss and sand to grow them in heavy clay areas, it might be easier to locate a nearby pick-your-own farm and pick and freeze what you need while they are in season. Of course, you must use the rabbiteye or rabbiteye hybrid varieties (high bush varieties are for northern gardens) in the southern kitchen garden, but don't worry—the quality is superb and production is outstanding. If you have the right soil, this is another fruit crop that is excellent for the organic gardener primarily because it has few pest or disease problems. Rabbiteye blueberries prefer an extremely acid, sandy soil (pH 4.5–5.8) with good drainage and abundant organic matter. Even when planting in sandy soils, incorporate a generous amount of organic peat at planting, and keep the blueberries heavily mulched. Blueberries are shallow rooted, requiring even moisture throughout the growing season. They also require cross-pollination, so it is important to plant more than one variety. Southern highbush, rabbiteyes, and hybrids are best for the lower South, and northern highbush varieties are best for the upper South.

Variety	Ripen	Type	Remarks/Description
Beckyblue	Late May	Rabbiteye	Plants are tall and vigorous. This is one of the earliest and best of the hybrid blueberries. Plant Aliceblue as a pollinator. Fruit is medium blue, medium in size with a small dry stem scar.
Bluecrop	June	Northern Highbush	This is perhaps the top variety for gardeners in the upper South. In fact, it is considered the standard of excellence. Upright, vigorous bush. Very productive. Large, firm, flavorful fruit does not drop or crack. Tolerates hot summers if soil is moist, acidic, and high in humus. Requires 800 chill hours. Self-fruitful. Upper South variety.
Blueray	June	Northern Highbush	Best variety for hot climates—assuming you have the cold winters needed to break dormancy. Large, firm fruit, excellent flavor. Upright, vigorous bush, very productive. Requires 800 chill hours. Self-fruitful. Upper South variety.
Brightwell	June	Rabbiteye	Plants are upright and spreading. The fruit is medium sized, medium blue, with a small dry stem scar. The blueberries are firm and separate easily.
Climax	May–late June	Rabbiteye	Plants are upright and spreading with a medium-sized fruit. Seeds are somewhat prominent resulting in a gritty texture.
Elliott	Late June	Northern Highbush	Heaviest-bearing variety and latest to ripen. Medium-size berries, slightly tart, will not crack or drop. Upright, vigorous bush. Tolerates hot summers if soil is moist, acidic, and high in humus. 800 hours. Self-fruitful. Upper South variety.
Garden Blue	May–late June	Rabbiteye	Small, good-quality berry. Ripens over a long period of time making it an excellent choice for home gardeners. A strong grower.
Magnolia	Early May	Southern Highbush	Medium-sized productive, vigorous plants with a spreading growth habit. Medium-sized fruit with good flavor, color, firmness, and small picking scar.

Variety	Ripen	Type	Remarks/Description
Ozarkblue	May	Northern/Southern Highbush Hybrid	Exceptional yields with good fruit size and quality. Recommended for planting in the upper part of the South because it requires 800–1,000 chill hours. Ozarkblue has consistently fruited when most other southern highbush and rabbiteye cultivars have had partial to total crop losses to spring freezes and frost. Pollinate with Summit.
Pearl River	Early May	Southern Highbush/Rabbiteye Hybrid	Vigorous, productive, upright plants. Pearl River is a hybrid of highbush and rabbiteye blueberries. Fruit is firm, medium-sized, good flavor, small scar, and somewhat darker than other cultivars.
Premier	Late May–June	Rabbiteye	Ripens two to three weeks before Tifblue. Large fruit with good flavor. Plants are vigorous, upright, disease resistant, and productive.
Powderblue	June–July	Rabbiteye	Plant is vigorous, disease resistant, and productive. Ripens similar to Tifblue with better fruit color and more foliage. Resists cracking in periods of excess rain.
Tifblue	June–July	Rabbiteye	Very vigorous upright plant with many suckers. Fruit is medium to large in size and light blue. Consistent, high-quality, high-yielding variety.
Southmoon	Late April–early May	Southern Highbush	Fruit is large, firm, good scar, medium color, and good flavor. Bush is vigorous and upright. Star is a good pollinator.
Star	Late April–early May	Southern Highbush	Fruit is large and easy to harvest because of a concentrated ripening period. Fruit has excellent scar, firmness, good color, and good flavor. The plant leafs strongly before the first flowers open. The recommended pollinator is Southmoon. Ripens April–May.
Summit	May	Southern Highbush	A mid- to late season (June–early July) southern highbush cultivar. Fruit is firm with large and excellent color, flavor, and picking scar. Resistant to cracking, tearing, and stemming. Plant is semiupright with medium vigor. Ozarkblue is a good pollinator.

Raspberries are best adapted to the upper South because they prefer a milder summer than is normally experienced along the coastal areas. All raspberries require a well-drained soil to avoid root rot. Black raspberries are especially susceptible to anthracnose and cane blight, and fruit size is also small. Black and purple raspberries also grow more vigorously and require more pruning than red-fruited cultivars. All canes of fall-fruiting or primocane-fruiting red raspberries are pruned just above the soil surface during the dormant season.

Most raspberries don't produce well in southern gardens but this Dormanred variety was bred for the South. As a fresh berry the flavor is bland for a raspberry, but when processed for jams or jellies it is rather good.

RASPBERRY VARIETIES

Variety	Harvest Season	Remarks/Description
Bababerry	May–June and September–December	A good-tasting red berry with a waxy bloom. Has produced excellent crops in Southern California.
Dorman Red	June	This is by far the strongest grower for the South. It is also a good producer, but the quality is poor. It is a red variety as are all of the raspberries that will grow in the lower South.
Heritage	September–December	Heritage an excellent producer for the upper South, especially during the fall season. If provided with afternoon shade, mulch, lots of fertilizer, and organic matter, it seems to have at least some potential for the lower South. It produces excellent-quality fruit.
Jewel	June	Black, medium-sized firm fruit with good flavor. Plants are cold hardy and productive under good care. Resistant to anthracnose fungus and more disease resistant than many black raspberries. For planting in the upper South.
Latham	June	Red, medium-sized, firm fruit of good quality. Good preserved or frozen. Upper South variety.
Redwing	September–December	An offspring of Heritage that would be worth trying for fall production in the South. Produces its fall crop of red fruit about 10 days later than Heritage. Fruit quality is slightly better than Heritage, and the plants are more heat resistant.
Royalty	June	Produces large purple fruit. More productive than red raspberry cultivars. Very susceptible to root rot.
San Diego	June–July and September–December	A Southern California variety worth trying in the South. Plants may be difficult to locate.

the southern kitchen garden

This butternut hybrid squash is typical of winter squash varieties with compact vines and excellent production. This high-quality squash is great for making pumpkin pies or for baking with butter and brown sugar.

Eggplants come in a variety of colors and shapes. Typically the green ones and the long, skinny ones have the most tender skins and nonbitter flesh with comparatively few seeds.

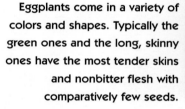

Homegrown sweet corn like this sweet gene hybrid (G 90) is a summer treat for gardeners with an oversize kitchen garden. Even in a small garden you can plant in blocks of three or more rows (to ensure good pollination) and enjoy this buttery golden delight.

Hot peppers come in many colors and sizes. The amount of heat varies too. They can be mildly hot like the long New Mexico chile, medium hot like the jalapeño, or fiery hot like the small, yellow chiles.

Swiss chard is little more than a beet with big leaves and no storage root but it will produce almost year-round. The leafy portion is tender and mild and the leaf petioles are delicious too. It can be used fresh in a salad or chopped up and sautéed. First fry some small bits of bacon and green onion. Add the chopped stems first—they need more cooking to make them tender—then add the leaves and cook until wilted. Finally add some balsamic vinegar, salt, and pepper. Now grab a fork, a piece of freshly buttered cornbread, and treat your taste buds to a kitchen garden delight.

This is the Adams kitchen garden in late spring. It is bursting with onions, brussels sprouts, kale, edible podded peas, potatoes, and herbs. Only a few steps from the front door, it doesn't take much imagination to plan a delicious and nutritious meal with this garden for inspiration.

This kitchen garden at the Antique Rose Emporium in Independence, Texas, is filled with Swiss chard, squash, flowers, and pots planted to kale, herbs, and more flowers.

Tomatoes are just one of the many fresh treats you can look forward to in your kitchen garden. From the tiny Texas Wild to the sandwich filling Goliath they make all the hard work worthwhile for tomato lovers. Just imagine your first BLT of the season—the acid sweetness of a vine-ripened tomato, the warm taste of bacon and crisp lettuce, a dollop of mayonnaise to marry the flavors, and toasted whole wheat bread. Who cares if you've spent $10 apiece on these tomatoes—they're worth it!

The kitchen garden in summer with containers filled with flowers, ornamental grasses, herbs, and bougainvillea. Almost too pretty to eat but inside the gate crookneck squash, zucchinis, bush beans, and golden wax beans beckon the cook to prepare an inspired dinner. Dust off the cookbooks. A legendary meal will make you the family hero tonight.

Onion chives flourish in cool weather and they last well into early summer when they become a bit ragged. Summer is the dormant season in the southern kitchen garden—we harvest some okra, a little climbing spinach, but mostly we yearn to vacation in Alaska. Don't worry though, the chives will return in the fall.

Apple blossoms signal spring with delicate pinks suffusing to white. Why not border the kitchen garden with dwarf fruit trees espaliered along the fence? If you have room plant a small orchard. Mulch around the trees to control weeds but plant wildflowers in the rows and celebrate the flowers and the bees while you contemplate a bountiful harvest—apple butter, peach jam, and all the good things that can come from the orchard

Mollie's Delicious apples in a Texas Hill Country garden. Makes you want to grab one and make it snap to your bite, savor the sweet, complex juices, and be thankful for the experience. Fruit crops require more attention and pest control but oh the rewards. Be sure to do some planning and select varieties adapted to your area.

Home mushroom production is not as far fetched as it might seem. Start with one of the prepared commercial kits like the one that produced these oyster mushrooms. This is a great project to get the children interested in food production and maybe provide some garden labor in the future. We all have the potential to be a mentor every day of our lives—it's an opportunity we shouldn't ignore.

Brian and Loraine Koehl's kitchen garden luxuriant with bush beans and tomatoes. In the background you can see the homemade greenhouse that Brian built. It's a great place to be on a cold winter day and they use it to start their tomato plants and to overwinter tropicals that would freeze outside.

Big Jim New Mexico chiles hanging red ripe on the plant, ready to harvest and you're ready for chiles on a burger—New Mexico style—or green chile stew or green chile enchiladas (in case you're wondering these chiles are also harvested green). Pop these beauties on a hot grill and turn them often to scald the skins which then pull off easily (after they cool) and freeze some for use in the winter while you're planning the next season's garden.

Compost piles aren't just for compost. This one at the Adams kitchen garden has an old fence gate attached—perfect for growing pole beans or cucumbers. Plants grow like Jack's bean stalk next to a compost pile. Hint: Use every inch of space you can find.

Plants like Gregg's Mist flower (*Eupatorium greggii*) draw butterflies to the garden like a magnet. The caterpillar stage may eat a few leaves— the pretty butterfly larvae seem to prefer weeds—but that's OK. This is one pest we can tolerate.

This Anna apple espaliered to a trellis makes a beautiful and tasty background to accent any garden setting. Anna and Dorsett Golden are two of the lowest chill requirement apples and they are best adapted to the lower South. Both are descendants of Golden Delicious and they make good pollinators for each other.

Corncockle and larkspur should be planted in the fall to add variety to the spring garden. Flowers are always welcome in the kitchen garden. Other cool season choices include calendulas, dianthus, snapdragons, pansies, petunias, and violas. In the summer garden plant zinnias, tithonia, sunflowers, gomphrena, moss rose, and other heat-loving flowers.

Brian and Loraine Koehl's summer kitchen garden—this time with a view of a trellis used to make the most of vertical space. Tomatoes, squash, beans, okra, and peppers are just some of the warm season vegetables that thrive in this garden.

A swallowtail butterfly sips nectar from the flowers of the Mexican marigold mint. Other good plants to attract butterflies to the garden include cilantro (allowed to flower), pentas, zinnias, lantana, and tithonia.

Byzantine glads will naturalize in the garden without becoming a pest. They usually develop a nice small clump 2–3 feet across. If they should begin to spread, your gardening friends would love to have a few corms to add to their gardens. After the foliage matures in early summer they die back to the soil, beginning their growth again in late winter. Be sure to locate them where they can remain perennial, though they can be moved in the dormant season, if necessary.

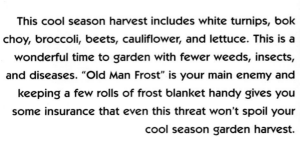

This cool season harvest includes white turnips, bok choy, broccoli, beets, cauliflower, and lettuce. This is a wonderful time to garden with fewer weeds, insects, and diseases. "Old Man Frost" is your main enemy and keeping a few rolls of frost blanket handy gives you some insurance that even this threat won't spoil your cool season garden harvest.

The summer herb harvest can be sizable. Some herbs like rosemary dry well—others like basil are better chopped or mixed in olive oil and frozen into cubes for use during the cold months when fresh basil would have to come from the greenhouse. Of course seasonality is the key, so gorge on basil pesto in the summer, use fresh rosemary twigs to brush barbecue sauce on grilling chicken, and substitute Mexican marigold mint for the hard-to-grow tarragon.

Jeri and Joe Guyton's kitchen garden is close to the house but it is only one of several kitchen gardens on this country estate. This garden concentrates on the "I need it right now" herbs, salad greens, onions, etc. The others were built as space was needed for sweet corn, eggplants, tomatoes, more sweet corn.

Sweet peas, planted in the fall, add color and a wonderful fragrance to the spring garden. You can't eat any part of this plant but you can pick to your heart's delight and fill your home with their sweet perfume.

Morning glories take over the trellis or fence for the summer after the sweet peas have faded. These plants grow rapidly and they come in a myriad of colors from heavenly blue to rose, brilliant red, and dark purple. Most aren't fragrant but the butterflies love them and you can always plant the fragrant, night blooming moonvine to attract big, gentle moths to your evening garden.

This peach tree has made one year of growth after being cut back to 24 inches at planting. This is the open center form of pruning and it works especially well with peaches and nectarines. The tree develops like an upside-down umbrella with 3–4 main scaffold limbs allowing good light penetration and the tree remains relatively small and easy to care for.

The same peach tree after the second year of growth. First remove diseased or crossing limbs, open up the center by removing half or more of the inward growing branches, and then tip back the main scaffold limbs to keep them under 7 feet. Tip other growing shoots about one-third. Hint: Most people don't remove enough wood.

This newly planted peach tree has been cut back to 24 inches and the small branches have been removed. As the tree makes growth, select 3–4 strong shoots near the top and evenly spaced around the trunk. These shoots will be left to grow but other shoots that sprout below will be pinched when 4–6 inches long to create a "trashy trunk." These "trashy" shoots will be removed in the next year or two but in the meantime they will protect the trunk and produce food to encourage rapid growth.

Each year peach and nectarine trees need to have one-third to one-half of the new growth removed to control the size of the tree and open it up for good light penetration (ensuring good fruit color). This pruning also makes it easier to spray for pests and the fruit will be easier to harvest.

Potatoes are about ready to harvest with kale and sprouting broccoli in the background. Close by, the Adams "barn style" house is only a few steps from the kitchen garden and its bountiful harvest.

It's late May in the Adams kitchen garden and the potatoes are being harvested. Zucchini and hybrid yellow crookneck squash are producing. Beans, both the pole and bush varieties, are coming along while the salad bed and herb bed are equally lush.

Strawberries are a fun crop in the kitchen garden. They are planted in the fall (Oct/Nov), harvested in the spring (April/May), and then dug out like a cool season vegetable crop. You'll still have time to plant bush beans in the bed before it gets too hot. Gardeners occasionally carry their strawberries through the summer but the buildup of spider mites and diseases often makes it impractical.

Nasturtiums aren't just a pretty addition to the cool season garden—they also make a wonderful sandwich. Pick a mix of tender leaves and flowers. Spread butter or cream cheese on whole wheat bread, combine, and munch.

Rabbiteye blueberries and the rabbiteye hybrids are ideally suited to the acid soil areas of the South. Even if you have a heavy clay soil that is a bit alkaline you can always grow them in raised beds with sandy soil mixed half and half with peat moss.

Johnny-jump-ups or violas are hardy in the fall garden. The prolific blooms are also edible. Plant them in October, expect a few blooms through the winter, and then get ready for a riot of color in the spring.

Zinnias like these large-flowered Benary Giants add color to the garden and they literally pull butterflies out of the sky. Zinnias also make a long-lasting cut flower for the table. Don't be afraid to buy the expensive hybrid seeds, the seedlings are easy to transplant and started plants may not be available. Just sow them in a short row where you have an open space in the garden. After they germinate and develop two sets of leaves use a plastic knife to separate and lift them out to their final spacing. Water carefully and daily—in a week it will look like you set them out as expensive transplants.

The spring kitchen garden with lettuce and onions in the foreground and tomatoes (in the lower garden) covered with fiber row cover to protect them from wind damage and light frosts.

The fall kitchen garden salad bed planted to a mix of lettuce, arugula, radicchio, purslane and other salad vegetables.

Spring Kitchen Garden

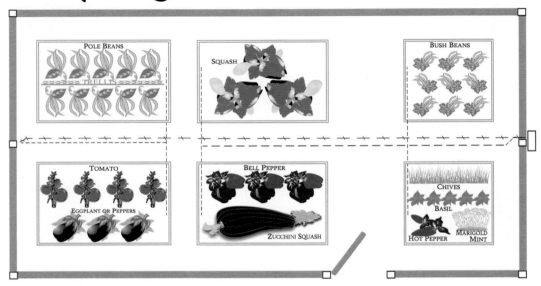

Fall Kitchen Garden

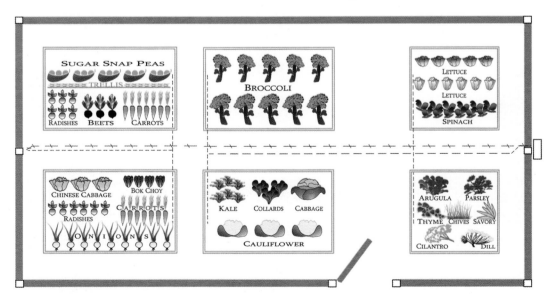

Illustrations by Nancy McClanahan, Montgomery County Master Gardener

Strawberries grow more like a vegetable than a big ol' bed-hogging fruit crop, so they are a natural for the kitchen garden. The trick is finding plants each year in the fall. Most southern gardeners will find that growing strawberries as an annual is the best way to go. If you can keep your spring-producing plants healthy through the summer, you can also select new plants each fall and pull the old ones plus extra new plants to leave the new crop spaced a foot apart each October/November. Otherwise, you will need to find a nursery that has new starts available each year in October/November. The reason for this annual renewal is to avoid the buildup of spider mites and diseases in the planting.

STRAWBERRY VARIETIES

Variety	Description
Chandler	Recommended for southern planting. This California variety has exceptional flavor and color for a southern variety. A vigorous, high-yielding variety. Due to lack of winter hardiness, not well suited for planting north of the Mid-Atlantic region. Chandler is also susceptible to anthracnose disease.
Redchief	Redchief is the old commercial variety, and it is still one of the "best all-around" berries. Its hardiness and resistance to red stele (root disease) makes it a consistent producer of medium to large firm fruit. Excellent variety for freezing. Although it is still widely planted, it has been steadily replaced by Honeoye and Jewel for commercial planting.
Seascape	The University of California breeding program released this variety in 1992. This day-neutral has been highly successful for northeastern growers for summer and fall production, but it also performs well in the South. Fruit is large and productive. The berries have good flavor when picked ripe from the plant.
Selva	The most widely planted variety in California and Florida, it produces huge berries that are seen in the grocery stores. When allowed to fully ripen on the plant, they can develop flavor, but the store-bought fruit is often tasteless or, at most, a bit sour. This California release has great yielding potential; however, it decreases in the eastern United States.
Sequoia	Earliest California variety and sweetest. Exceptional taste, productivity, and pest resistance; the most popular variety with home gardeners.

Nectarines

See peaches.

NECTARINE VARIETIES

Variety	Chill Requirement (hours)	Ripe/Color	Remarks/Description
Double Delight	300–500	July. Dark red, yellow-fleshed freestone.	Attractive semidouble pink flowers, plus good-quality fruit, makes this an excellent tree for homeowners. May produce excessive double fruit that needs to be removed during the thinning process.
Fantasia	650–750	Late July. Red over yellow, yellow-fleshed freestone.	Wonderful flavor but unattractive fruit. Mid- to upper South variety.
Juneglo	700	Mid July. Red with some russeting. Semifreestone.	Fruits have 10%–15% split pits and varying fruit size. Mid- to upper South variety.
Karla Rose	600–700	June. Mostly red, yellow-fleshed clingstone.	Good quality but very small unless thinned a lot. Some disease problems. Mid-South variety.
Mayglo	500–600	Late May. Red, yellow-fleshed cling.	Fair to good quality. Nice round shape, burgundy red color.
Necta Zee Miniature	500	Mid-June–early July. Yellow freestone with red skin.	Sweet, very flavorful fruit. Strong, vigorous tree to 6 feet. Best self-fruitful miniature nectarine.
Redgold	850	Late July. Skin 80%–90% red with freestone yellow flesh.	Fruit are large with high-quality and firm flesh. This tree is a vigorous grower. Upper South variety.
Snow Queen	700–800	Early to mid-June. Dull red over pale yellow, white-flesh.	Extemely high-quality, clingstone fruit. Not a pretty nectarine but large with unforgettable flavor. Upper South variety.
Sun Glo	850	Late July. Red/yellow, yellow-fleshed freestone.	Large, round, and pretty. Great taste. Upper South variety.
Sunmist	400	Good size; blooms early so it may be less susceptible to plum curculio.	Vigorous, healthy tree.

Peaches

Peaches (nectarines) are one of the more challenging fruits to grow; however, it's easy to keep these trees "sized down" for the kitchen garden. You can plant genetic dwarfs, or you can dwarf standard-size trees with a pruning saw. The key is to start at planting. Genetic dwarfs need to be cut back by one-third, but standard trees need to be pruned back to 24 to 42 inches—even if you bought the "premium" 6- to 8-foot tree.

Homegrown peaches are so much better than the ones at the grocery store because they can be left to ripen fully before harvest. Anything this luscious attracts a few pests. Expect to spray stone fruit crops (peaches, plums, and nectarines) if you want fruit that isn't infected with brown rot or wormy.

This will ensure that three to four main scaffold limbs will originate low to the ground, giving you an "upside-down umbrella" shape that is easy to prune, spray, and pick from. Also be sure to remove small twiggy limbs when you plant to encourage strong, new shoots to develop. Genetic dwarfs tend to grow as low-branching, dense shrubs, so they don't need a lot of yearly pruning—just prune out crossing branches and cut them back to 5 to 6 feet each year.

Fresh Peach Cobbler

2 large peaches, peeled and sliced
½ cup sugar, divided
½ cup butter or margarine, melted
1 cup all-purpose flour

2 tsp. baking powder
¼ tsp. salt
dash ground nutmeg
¾ cup milk

In a bowl, combine peaches and ¾ cup sugar; set aside. Pour butter into an 8-inch-square baking pan. In a bowl, combine flour, baking powder, salt, nutmeg, and remaining sugar; stir in milk just until combined. Pour over butter. Top with the peaches. Bake at 375° degrees for 45 to 50 minutes or until golden brown. Yield: 8 servings.

---

the fruit garden

Most peaches and nectarines are also self-fertile, so you only need one tree if that is all you have room for. Factor in beautiful flowers and you have a great small tree or shrub for the kitchen garden. Scale insects, borers, and bacterial canker may take these trees out in 6 to 8 years, but just replant—the fruit is worth it. Before you buy your first peach or nectarine tree, take into account that they require perfect drainage. Even very short periods of water-saturated soil can cause tree death. They are also affected by a number of serious disease and insect problems, which means they require frequent and regular applications of an insecticide and fungicide. This is not a good fruit for the organic gardener. Also these trees should be planted in full sun. It is usually not necessary to plant more than one variety because most peaches are self-fruitful. Nemaguard is the most common rootstock, but it probably isn't needed in heavy clay soils since nematodes aren't much of a problem here. A new rootstock that shows promise is Cadaman. Two semidwarfing rootstocks to look for are Controller 5 (USC-Davis) and VV-1 (Raintree Nursery).

PEACH VARIETIES

Variety	Chill Requirement (hours)	Ripe/Color	Remarks/Description
Elberta	800	Late July–early August. Yellow flesh.	Classic freestone with rich, peach flavor; high scoring in taste tests. Use fresh, canned, and cooked. Self-fruitful. Upper South only.
Flordaking	450	Mid-May. Yellow flesh.	Earliest peach in this listing. Large fruit. Poor quality. Dry spring may improve flavor some years. Clingstone. The University of Florida has released a tremendous number of low- to medium-chill peach and nectarine varieties in the last 10 years. This variety is probably the best known, and if the rest were no better, we would have to question the waste of taxpayers' funds in this effort. Fortunately, most are better, but you have to wonder: don't the plant breeders taste this stuff?
Golden Jubilee	800	July. Yellow flesh (red at pit). Skin one-third blushed with mottled red.	Favorite cold-country peach for canning and fresh eating. Derived from Elberta. Medium-sized, oblong, freestone. Self-fruitful. Upper South variety.
GulfPrince	400	Late May–Early June. Yellow.	Large clingstone variety with good color.
Honey Babe Miniature Peach	500	Early to mid-July. Yellow freestone.	Sweet, rich peach flavor. Heavy bearing 5-foot tree. Excellent choice for home orchard or container. Self-fruitful.

the southern kitchen garden

Variety	Chill Requirement (hours)	Ripe/Color	Remarks/Description
Juneprince	600–700	Mid-June. Red blush over yellow, yellow flesh, semifreestone.	One of the highest-flavored varieties for this season. Round shape with a small nipple.
La Feliciana	550–600	Late June. Yellow-fleshed freestone.	Has been widely tested in the South. Quality is good to excellent. Delta (needs a pollinator like White Robin peach or Suncoast nectarine), Gala, and Regal are new releases from LSU.
Loring	750–800	Early–mid July. Large yellow freestone.	Superb, large yellow freestone. Excellent flavor and texture, low acid. Harvests over 2- to 3-week period. Requires little or no thinning. Excellent for home orchard.
Mid-Pride	300–400	Mid–late June. Yellow-orange with distinctive red striping, yellow-fleshed freestone.	One of the few California varieties that shows promise for the South. Good tree vigor, average to good fruit quality. Blooms later than many other low-chill varieties.
Pix Zee Miniature Peach	500	Mid- to late June. Yellow with red over orange skin.	Delicious, firm freestone. Vigorous miniature perfect for small spaces growing to 6-foot Self-fruitful.
Ranger	900–950	Early July. Large yellow freestone.	One of the best late-blooming/frost-hardy peaches for cold climates. Full-flavored, high-quality yellow freestone.
Red Baron	500–600	Mid-June–early July. Yellow with red blush. Yellow-fleshed semifreestone.	Beautiful pinkish-red, semidouble flowers, and high-quality fruit that ripens over an extended harvest period.
Redskin	700–800	Mid- to late July. Red over yellow. Yellow-fleshed freestone.	Very high quality. Long bloom period. Upper South variety. New varieties for this region include Encore and Bounty.
Sentinel	650–750	Early to mid-June. Dark red blush over yellow. Yellow-fleshed, semicling.	Excellent-quality fruit, good flavor and texture. Very productive, resistant to bacterial leaf spot. Upper South variety.
Surecrop	1,000	Mid- to late June, yellow cling.	Semifreestone with tender flesh and rich flavor. Ripens 43 days before Elberta. Upper South only.
Suwannee	650	July/early August. Yellow fruit. Yellow-gold flesh with red markings around pit. Freestone.	Excellent quality, attractive fruit for the late season.
Tex Royal	600	Mid- to late June. Bright yellow with	A recent release from Texas A&M University. High quality with a good

(*continued*)

Variety	Chill Requirement (hours)	Ripe/Color	Remarks/Description
		red blush. Yellow-fleshed, freestone.	rounded form. Better quality than the semiclingstone variety Texstar.
Tropic Snow	200	Mid-June. White flesh.	Delicious freestone for mild winter climates. Balanced acid and sugar, superb flavor. Showy blossoms. From Florida, introduced in 1988. Very low winter chilling requirement. Self-fruitful.
Tropic Sweet	150	May. Yellow freestone.	You may lose these low-chill varieties some years because of a late spring freeze but they are good insurance for mild winter years.
UFO	250	May. Yellow flesh.	Flying saucer, Peento-type peach with firm yellow flesh and unique shape.

Pears

Pears are a traditional southern fruit. If varieties with resistance to bacterial fire blight are selected, then they become a good choice for the organic gardener. As with apples, it is important to plant more than one variety in order to get good cross-pollination and fruit set. Pear trees can grow 25 to 30 feet tall and half as wide, so allow them plenty of space. Fortunately, they are adapted to a wide range of soil types as long as the drainage is adequate. Try to avoid wet spots or low-lying areas. Anticipate that trees will generally take 5 to 7 years to come into production.

The quince rootstock typically used for dwarfing pears doesn't do well in heavy soils, so in many areas of the South, you may have to settle for a tree on callery (*Pyrus calleryana*) rootstock and keep it in bounds with pruning and branch spreading. You can't do too much pruning, however, or you will encourage vigorous growth and fire blight infection. Branch spreading is discussed in the section on training fruit trees, but it essentially involves using spreaders or weights to pull down and widen the limb to trunk angle resulting in earlier and heavier production.

Pears benefit from cross-pollination, but specific information on compatible southern varieties is lacking. Varieties like Pineapple have a reputation for being good pollinators, but most varieties—if they bloom at the same time—should pollinate each other. Pears are one of the easiest fruit trees to propagate by budding or grafting, so it is easy to graft a pollinator limb into your favorite pear tree and ensure good fruit set. There are also lots of ornamental pears in adjacent landscapes that can serve as pollinators. Don't fret if you only have room for one pear tree in your kitchen garden—pollination may be only a neighbor's yard away, or you can graft in a different variety.

Variety	Chill Requirement (hours)	Ripe/Color	Remarks/Description
Acres Home	300–400	August. Light green to yellow.	Chance seedling, high quality, and resistance to fire blight. Not readily available.
Ayres	600–800	August. Brown russet and red blush.	Excellent dessert quality, although not as good as Warren. Medium-sized fruit. Highly resistant to fire blight. Slow to begin bearing.
Kieffer	300–400	September–October. Yellow, rough skin with some blush.	Large, coarse pear used mainly for canning. Stores well. Slight musty flavor which adds character to pear butter and other foods. Tolerates fire blight.
Le Conte	300–400	August. Attractive yellow pear.	Above-average, fresh-eating quality, rather susceptible to fire blight. Typical pear shape.
Leona	300–400	August. Yellow with some blush.	Popular in south Louisiana and slightly susceptible to fire blight.
Magness	800	August. Pale green.	Excellent dessert quality with medium-sized fruit similar to Warren. Highly resistant to fire blight. Upper South variety.
Maxine	800	August to early September. Green with red blush.	Very good dessert quality with medium to large, attractive fruit. Good to fair fire blight resistance. Reported to be the same pear as Starking Delicious. Upper South variety.
Meadows	400	August. Yellow-green with some blush.	Sturdy, erect tree with fruit that has a nice winey flavor with ripening.
Orient	300–400	August. Yellow and somewhat russetted.	Hard, large, round pear of fair to good quality with good blight resistance. Best for processing.
Pineapple	150	August. Large yellow fruit.	Reported to have a pineapple-like flavor. Store for fresh use or use for processing. Fruit is large unless tree is allowed to overbear.
Southern Bartlett	400	August. Yellow.	Similar to Southern Queen.
Southern Queen	200–400	August. Yellow.	High-quality pyriform fruit with excellent resistance to fire blight.
Tenn. (Tennessee)	200–400	August. Red blush with some russeting.	Medium-sized and somewhat rounded bell shape. Shows good blight resistance and has good- to excellent-quality fruit. Rather susceptible to fungal leaf spot and premature defoliation.
Warren	600–800	August. Pale green. Not russeted.	Very high-quality fruit. Trees are slow to begin bearing (1–15 years), and leaf spot can be severe. Resistant to fire blight.

Plums, Apricots, and Cherries

Of these three, plums have the most potential, and even they may be questionable due to their susceptibility to bacterial canker. In northern regions cherries may be quite tempting; and in dry climates—or with lots of spraying for brown rot fungus—apricots are luscious when harvested ripe from the tree. All three require cross-pollination, and this is often a problem. Finding one variety adapted to your region is difficult enough; finding two good ones may prove daunting, especially with apricots and cherries. Even though there are a number of plums we can grow, the blooming periods must overlap and they must produce viable pollen. The Bruce plum, for example, blooms its head off but doesn't produce viable pollen, and the fruit it produces is barely edible. A promising new variety from the University of Florida—Gulf Blaze—blooms so early it is essential to plant one of the other varieties from this series like Gulf Beauty to ensure pollination.

In a good year plums can be extremely productive. They do require spraying, however, and pollination can be a problem. Unlike peaches, which are self-fertile, plums require cross-pollination. Just be sure to plant varieties that bloom at the same time and you should get a good fruit set.

the southern kitchen garden

Apricots are so scrumptious ripe from the tree that it is hard not to consider growing them. Unfortunately, they are very susceptible to brown rot fungus, cracking from uneven moisture supply, and it is hard to find quality varieties with the correct chill requirement. Gardeners keep trying though. Your best bet is to check with local growers, nurseries, and the county agent to see if there have been local successes. Generally, they are better in a dry climate, but since you can rarely buy quality apricots at the store, you just have to keep trying and keep the sprayer handy. Some of the varieties often recommended for the South include Goldkist, Katy, Blenheim, Royal, and Lorna.

Cherries are even more elusive—especially in the mid- to lower South. Stella is a low-chill, self-fertile variety often suggested for trial; and of course there are semitropical varieties like the Capulin cherry, but they produce fruit that is mostly seed, and the trees often die of root rot in southern gardens. Nanking bush cherries will produce from the upper Gulf Coast–north, but they, too, are mostly seed. Gardeners in the upper South can give sour cherries like Montmorency a try, or go crazy and plant sweet cherries like Stella and Black Gold. If they produce, be sure you have a good pair of binoculars for bird-watching because the birds will love you.

Plums are much more forgiving than peaches or nectarines. Plums will benefit from an occasional application of insecticide and fungicide, but they do not require as many applications as peaches or nectarines. A few varieties are self-fruitful, but most will benefit by having a pollinator present. The biggest problem facing plum growers in southern kitchen gardens is bacterial canker. This disease is fatal. Best control can be achieved by cleaning all pruning equipment prior to and after pruning each tree with 10% chlorine bleach. The disease is primarily spread through pruning cuts. It is also important to spray stone fruits (including plums) with a copper fungicide in the fall (October/November). This will knock the leaves off but the copper residue will help to reduce infection through bud scars where the leaves have fallen. Be sure not to use these copper fungicides during the growing season as the foliage will be severely damaged. Plum leaf scald is a bacterial disease that causes a plugging of the vascular tissue. Initial symptoms are yellowing and browning of the leaf tips, followed by shoot dieback and eventually death of the tree. Leafhopper insects are the apparent vector. Planting resistant varieties and removing wild plum trees (a possible source of infection) are about the only solutions to this serious problem. Brown rot fungus—usually recognized as decaying, eventually mummified fruit—is another major disease that will require spraying with a fungicide for prevention.

Variety	Chill Requirement (hours)	Ripe/Color	Remarks/Description
Au-Series— Au-Producer	500–700	Ripen June/July. Dark red skin and red flesh.	Auburn releases with resistance to leaf scald. They all ripen mid-June.
Au-Roadside		Magenta fruit with red flesh.	
Au-Rosa		Red fruit with some light yellow areas.	
Au-Rubrum		Maroon with red flesh.	
Beauty	300	May–early June. Reddish purple with yellow flesh.	Like most Japanese varieties developed in California, it is susceptible to leaf spot and leaf scorch. Fruit quality is good.
Green Gage	500	Ripens in August/September. Blue-purple with yellow-green flesh.	European plum, later blooming than Santa Rosa and other Japanese types. Longtime favorite for dessert, cooking, canning. Tender, juicy, rich flavor. Relatively small tree.
Gulf Series—	200	Ripen late May–June.	This Florida series offers a lot of potential for gardeners in the lower South. They are low chill and bloom very early, so it is often necessary to have several in the series planted to ensure pollination. Other early-blooming Japanese-type plums may also serve as pollinators.
Gulfbeauty		Reddish purple with yellow flesh.	
Gulfruby		Red to purple with yellow flesh.	
Gulfblaze		Dark red becoming purple with orange flesh.	
Gulfgold		Yellow with sweet, soft yellow flesh,	
Gulfrose		Dark, reddish purple with red flesh.	
Mariposa	200–300	June. Greenish bronze, with burgundy red flesh.	Excellent-quality fruit; unfortunately, it is not very pretty. It is a California variety, but the trees stay fairly healthy when planted in the South.
Methley	200	May. Small, reddish purple fruit, burgundy flesh color.	Excellent quality but rapidly develops a jellylike texture when too ripe. Self-fertile. Good disease tolerance.
Morris	600–700	Ripens in June. Red with red flesh.	Fair to good quality. Production has been erratic probably due to pollination problems. Upper South variety

Variety	Chill Requirement (hours)	Ripe/Color	Remarks/Description
Ozark Premier	700–800	June. Large red fruit with some yellow skin color, yellow flesh.	If thinned properly, this can be one of the largest plums grown. It has excellent quality and is somewhat self-fertile. Upper South variety.
Robusto	600	Ripens in June. Red skin and red flesh.	Fruit of medium firmness. Dependable crops. Excellent tree health.
Santa Rosa	400	Ripens in June. Purplish red, flesh yellow with red near skin.	An excellent-quality fruit. Susceptible to bacterial canker. Fairly self-fertile and a good pollinator for other varieties.

OTHER FRUITS AND A FEW NUTS

Don't limit yourself to the traditional fruit crops. Even huge trees like the pecan may fit in some garden plans—though usually as a separate orchard addition to the main kitchen garden. Others like citrus, figs, pomegranates, and jujubes are a natural. They can be the specimen plants in your kitchen garden.

Citrus

Citrus trees are a natural in the kitchen garden. They are attractive, evergreen trees with fragrant flowers and decorative fruit. The hardiest species can be planted in the ground in protected areas, and any of the smaller citrus species—especially lemons, limes, kumquats, and satsumas—can be grown in large containers on decks or patios. Citrus trees have relatively few problems, which makes them an excellent selection for organic gardeners. Scale and white fly are the major pests, which can be controlled with one of the many horticultural oils currently on the market. Citrus leaf miner is a relatively new pest that may require pesticides, or predators/parasites may eventually do the job. Most citrus species do not require a pollinator. Pruning is only required to maintain the shape and size desired. The less you prune, the more the trees will produce. It is especially critical with young trees that you remove the small fruits for 2 to 3 years. Otherwise, the plants can be severely stunted. Also, anticipate that the quality of fruits will improve as the trees get older—at least for a few years—then quality should remain consistent.

Variety	Cold Tolerance (degrees F)	Remarks/Description
Grapefruit	26–28	Bloomsweet is a slip-skin, white-fleshed grapefruit that is somewhat cold hardy. Henderson is the hardiest of the red-fleshed varieties. Rio Red, Ray Ruby, and Ruby Star are excellent-quality red varieties but less cold hardy than Henderson.
Kumquats	20–24	Meiwa and Changshou are the preferred varieties. They are round with few seeds, and both are much sweeter than Nagami. Nagami is an elongated fruit and the one most commonly found at the supermarket.
Other Mandarins	22–28	Clementine mandarin is currently one of the most popular mandarins in the world. The flesh is bright orange, finely textured, sweet, and juicy. Fairchild mandarin is a hybrid of Clementine mandarin and Orlando tangelo. Others worth noting include Changsha tangerine, Ponkan, Pon Koa, and Page.
Satsuma	20–24	Satsumas are the most commonly grown mandarins (tangerine-like fruit) in the lower South. They have slip skins and excellent-quality flesh. Varieties include: Brown Select, Kimbrough, Kisu, Miho, Owari, Okitsu, Seto, Armstrong Early, and others. Many are excellent early in the fall while the skins are still green or partially green.
Sweet Oranges	25–28	Republic of Texas is the hardiest of the sweet oranges. The fruit is sweet and mild but somewhat seedy. Cara Cara navel orange is a natural dwarf variety with deep pink flesh. It is similar to the darkest of the red grapefruit varieties. Moro blood orange is the most common of the pigmented oranges marketed in the United States. The fruit is round, of moderate size, and frequently borne in clusters. Moro is the most highly colored of the blood oranges, though Tarocco may have better flavor. All blood oranges are best grown in the lower South.
Sour Fruits	18–28	The Thomasville citrangequat makes an attractive tree with small, ornamental yellow to orange fruit. The fruit is sour, has slip skin, and is very good for lemonade-type drinks, especially while the fruits are still green to yellow. The flesh becomes rather dry by the time the fruit ripens to orange. Limequat and lemonquat will require some protection from the cold during most winters even in the lower South. In the upper South they are strictly a greenhouse- or container-grown and frost-protected crop. Ponderosa lemon produces a huge fruit that makes excellent lemonade. Meyer lemon produces a normal-size fruit in abundance. Both these citrus will require some protection even in the lower South, and they are probably best in pots so that they can be protected. The sunquat has very sweet skin and a sour, juicy flesh—it could have been called the "marmalade fruit" since it makes excellent marmalade. Compared with lemons, it is relatively hardy.

the southern kitchen garden

Birds Are "Winged Death" When It Comes to Figs and Most Other Fruit

Fresh figs are wonderful—just ask the birds. They may be easy to grow, but try getting them to the table. Most folks allow the birds to take a few, but the party can quickly get out of hand. And it's not just the mockingbirds you have to worry about—woodpeckers will attack figs, as will a number of other protected birds. That rules out the "12-gauge and number 9 shot" solution. Plus, picking lead shot out of your fruit is tedious.

So, in desperation, gardeners usually turn to bird netting. The trick is to wait until just before the fruit begins to ripen—actually, timing the application when the fruit approaches full size is a good idea since the birds will peck it and cause it to ripen early. Get a friend or two to help. Using sturdy bamboo poles—the 1-inch diameter work best—lift the netting over the tree and secure it around the trunk. I don't know how, but some small birds always seem to get under the net, so each day you will need to scold and release the captive birds while picking your figs. While birds particularly like figs, they like all of the same fruits that we do.

City birds are especially fond of fresh fruit. For one thing, there's a shortage of fresh fruit in the city, and there may be a stress factor that makes them crave "forbidden" fruits.

Don't get in a hurry to net your fruit trees. If you put the netting on too soon, the tree will grow through it and you will have permanent netting—ugly and ineffective at protecting next year's crop, which will be above the netting.

Figs

Figs can provide a real fresh fruit treat in the kitchen garden. They need virtually no spraying since they are relatively free from disease and insect pests, so this is another excellent crop for the organic gardener. The few pests that bother figs are minor and include fig rust, which causes leaf spot and late summer defoliation, and fruit souring from the dried fruit beetle. Fig rust, you'll probably just have to ignore or try a copper fungicide applied early in the season. The answer to fruit souring is to plant varieties with a closed eye or ones that develop with a drop of honey in the eye. Nematodes are a potential problem with figs. Thesemicroscopic roundworms attack the root system and cause slow growth, possible leaf drop, and nutrient deficiency symptoms. Nematodes are mostly a problem in sandy soils and not

The Celeste fig is hard to beat—the flavor is superb with a rich aftertaste and the closed eye ensures that the dried fruit beetle won't cause the fruit to sour. This variety produces its best figs on last year's wood so only prune it back a third each year.

much of a concern in heavy clay soils. Regardless, there are no nematicides for the home garden, so mulching with compost or "strawy manure" (not too strong, in other words) will help relieve this problem. Organic matter tends to encourage beneficial organisms that can reduce the number of nematodes in the soil. Figs also demand a lot of water. Be sure to water them thoroughly during dry periods, especially when the trees are loaded up with fruit.

FIG VARIETIES

Variety	Ripe/Color	Remarks/Description
Alma	Late June. Light yellow.	Fair quality, fruit has a drop of honey in the eye, reducing damage from the fruit beetle.
Celeste	June–July. Purplish brown.	Still probably the best-quality fig grown in the South. It has a complex sweetness and leaves a pleasant aftertaste. It also has a closed eye. Unfortunately, it is somewhat susceptible to cold and normally bears on last year's wood. A hard freeze or overzealous pruning can destroy the coming season's crop.
Excel	August. Yellow with amber flesh produces some "honey" in the eye.	One of many varieties developed by Ira Condit in California. Others to consider include Deanna (yellow with red pulp), Tena (yellow with light red pulp), and Yvonne (greenish yellow with white pulp).
Green Ischia	July–August. Green with red flesh.	Good-quality fruit but the tree is only moderately productive. The eye is partially closed, so the fruit beetle is not too damaging, and the green color is less attractive to birds.
LSU Purple	July–August. Purple with red flesh.	A Louisiana variety that produces very attractive large, purple, closed-eye figs on vigorous upright plants. This variety produces a good crop of figs on new growth, so it can be pruned heavily. Other LSU varieties to consider include LSU Gold and LSU Everbearing.
Texas Everbearing	July–August. Brown with amber flesh.	Large fig with a closed eye. Best for preserves. Produces on current season's growth. Usually produces two crops per season.
Violette de Bordeaux (Bordeaux, Negronne)	July–August. Almost black with red pulp.	Richly flavored with slight acidity. Early fruit (Brebas—produced on last year's growth) are large; later figs are small.

Grapes

Grapes are another natural for the kitchen garden. They are easy to grow on a trellis, or you can design an arbor for them to grow on—providing shade and a bountiful fruit crop. Most southern gardens are best adapted to muscadine grapes. They flourish in sandy, acid soils and produce heavily with a minimum of care. However, bunch grapes with resistance to Pierce's disease can also be grown. Grapes demand attention to training and trellis support, and they need regular applications of fungicide if regular production is expected. Unfortunately, the frequent use of pesticides may interfere with vegetable crops that need regular harvesting so be careful where you locate the vineyard. One of the biggest problems facing grape growers in the southeastern United States is Pierce's disease. If you decide to grow susceptible varieties, be prepared for grape plants to be relatively short lived. Generally the better-quality grapes are susceptible to Pierce's disease, limiting production to a few wine and jelly varieties. All commercial bunch grapes are self-fruitful.

Muscadine grapes are ideally suited to the southeastern United States This Ison variety is one of the self-fertile types. There are some great "female flowers only" varieties like Hunt and Scuppernong, just be sure to include some self-fertile varieties in your planting to ensure good pollination.

the fruit garden

Variety	Pierce's Resistance	Color/Type	Remarks/Description
Black Spanish (Lenoir)	Resistant	Black/seeded	Very productive variety for wine or jelly production. Fresh or "table grape" quality is poor. Plants are vigorous and easily managed.
Blanc du Bois	Resistant	White/seeded	This variety is capable of producing award-winning wines. It is especially susceptible to anthracnose. Not recommended for fresh eating.
Champanel	Resistant	Black/seeded	Small clusters of large, poor-quality grapes utilized primarily for wine and jelly. An excellent variety for arbors because it is very vigorous and disease resistant.
Favorite	Resistant	Blue-black/seeded	Apparently a seedling of Black Spanish with larger grapes and grape clusters and a slightly better quality.
Jupiter	Susceptible	Reddish blue to blue/seedless	One of the best of the blue table grapes released from University of Arkansas. It produces medium to large clusters of large thin-skinned grapes with excellent flavor and 20% soluble solids. Other blue releases include: Mars, Sunbelt, and Venus. All are best adapted to the mid- and upper South.
Lake Emerald	Resistant	Green/seeded	This variety has large fruit clusters, but only moderate production. Good disease resistance.
Neptune	Susceptible	Green/seedless	This Arkansas release produces large clusters of medium-size green berries with a fruity, pleasant flavor and 19.7% soluble solids. Upper South variety.
Red Flame	Susceptible	Reddish pink/seedless	A good-flavored, very popular table grape. Ruby Seedless is another high-quality red table grape similar to but more productive than Red Flame.
Reliance	Susceptible	Pink/seedless	This is the highest rated in flavor of the Arkansas varieties with up to 24% soluble solids. The clusters are medium to large, with small to medium berries. Another reddish-pink variety from Arkansas is Saturn.
Verdelet (Seibel 2110)	Moderate resistance	White/partially seedless	One of the early French hybrids. It produces a yellow-gold dessert-quality wine. Fair quality as a fresh grape.

Grapes, Muscadines

Muscadines are native to much of the southeastern United States. In the last 50 years, numerous new varieties have become available to growers, and tremendous strides have been made in quality including improved color, higher sugar content, and thinner skins. There has even been the development of seedless varieties though, to date, production is lacking. It should be noted that some muscadine varieties produce only female flowers and must be planted with self-fruitful varieties to ensure good pollination. There are far too many varieties to discuss them all. Those listed in the table are either well-known standard varieties or new, high-quality varieties with exceptional merit.

MUSCADINE VARIETIES

Variety	Female/Self-Fertile	Color/% Sugar	Remarks/Description
Black Beauty	Female	Black/23%	A very large-fruited variety with an edible skin. The large fruits ripen uniformly, produced in large clusters. This is one of the best black varieties.
Black Fry	Female	Black/19%	A very productive, good-quality grape that produces large clusters that ripen uniformly. Ripens early to midseason.
Carlos	Self-fertile	Bronze/16%	This grape is medium size, of good quality, and ripens early to midseason. It is very productive and excellent for wine making.
Cowart	Self-fertile	Black/17%	This variety has excellent flavor, large clusters of medium-size grapes. It is very productive and ripens early in the season.
Darlene	Female	Bronze/22%	The best of the bronze muscadines. It consistently produces large high-quality fruit on vigorous vines.
Fry	Female	Bronze/21%	A high-quality large fruit that produces large clusters. This variety ripens over a long period of time.
Hunt	Female	Black/17%	This older variety produces medium-size grapes in large clusters. It is a good-quality variety excellent for jams, jelly, and cold-pressed juice and wine. Ripens early in the season.
Ison	Self-fertile	Black/19%	A very productive, uniform ripening variety, producing large clusters of black grapes, early to midseason.

(continued)

Variety	Female/Self-Fertile	Color/% Sugar	Remarks/Description
Jumbo	Female	Black/15%	A very good-quality grape if allowed to fully ripen. Jumbo produces a vigorous vine and ripens early to midseason.
Pam	Female	Bronze/21%	Pam has the largest clusters of grapes in production. It is the heaviest-producing female variety. It has an edible skin, dry scar, and good disease resistance.
Rosa	Female	Pinkish Red/18%	Rosa is the best of the red grapes. It produces very sweet, good-quality grapes on a very vigorous vine. Excellent for home use.
Scuppernong	Female	Bronze/17%	Scuppernong is known all over for its strong, distinctive muscadine flavor. It produces small clusters of medium-size grapes in midseason.
Southern Home	Self-fertile	Black	This is a hybrid of bunch and muscadine grapes developed in Florida. It has unique oak-shaped leaves and is recommended for use in gardens for its fruit and aesthetic value. Fruit is muscadine-like, medium sized, and has good flavor and quality. Productivity is moderate.
Summit	Female	Red/20%	This older variety has excellent quality and production.

Pecans

Pecans and other nut crops really have no place in the kitchen garden. They take up too much space, and pecan and black walnut trees contain a substance called juglone that inhibits the growth of other plants. They also require frequent applications of a fungicide, insecticide, and zinc. It is generally recommended that homeowners plant the most disease-resistant varieties available, plan on growing them only for landscape purposes, and then count on production only in those years when environmental conditions are favorable. Suffice it to say that pecans are well adapted to the South, as are black walnuts. While they may not fit in the kitchen garden, they may have a place in other areas of larger landscapes. Chinese chestnuts, English walnuts, and pistachios might also be a potential crop for some areas of the South, but they all need to be tried in an orchard situation separate from the kitchen garden. Varieties listed here were selected primarily for their disease resistance, not nut size or quality. You need to plant both an early and late pollen-release variety to ensure good cross-pollination.

Variety	Pollen Release	Harvest/% Kernel/ Nuts per Pound	Remarks/Description
Caddo	Early	Early/50%/60–70	One of the most scab-resistant varieties currently available. Only average production of small football-shaped nuts.
Candy	Late	Early/48%/66	Produces small but very high-quality nuts. Has good disease resistance.
Choctaw	Late	Midseason/ 55%–60%/35–40	Choctaw is a very popular variety although it tends to split during harvest. It has good scab resistance and an attractive kernel.
Elliot	Late	Early/55%/40	Elliot is considered to be one of the most disease-resistant varieties for the Southeast. It produces small but very high-quality, light-colored kernels. Trees are slow to begin producing but produce a consistent crop once old enough.
Forkert	Late	Midseason/60%/50	High-quality kernels and good disease resistance are this variety's chief attributes.
Jackson	Early to self-fertile	Midseason/60%/42	This is a large pecan with high quality and good scab resistance. Yields are about half what a good commercial variety produces so as a result, it is primarily used for home production.
Kiowa	Late	Midseason/ 55%–60%/40–50	This variety has good disease resistance and large nut size. Trees are productive at a young age.
Melrose	Late	Midseason/55%/55	This variety has excellent resistance to pecan scab. It produces high-quality nuts with excellent size and color. The nuts are somewhat pointed at both ends.
Oconee	Early	Early/54%/48	This variety was released because of its large size, good production, high quality, and easily cracked kernel. Oconee will require fungicide sprays to control scab. Trees produce at an early age.
Pawnee	Early	Early/55%–60%/ 55–60	A large, high-quality pecan that produces on young trees. Potential for high yields on a tree with some disease resistance and apparent aphid resistance.
Sumner	Late	Midseason/ 50%–55%/55–60	This variety comes into production at an early age, producing medium-sized nuts with good disease resistance and excellent quality.
Surprise	Early	Midseason/49%/ 40–45	A seedling from Alabama, this variety has good scab resistance and consistent production even in bad years.

Mayhaws are famous in the South for the wonderful jellies and syrups that can be made from them. They are too tart to eat fresh but this tartness gives the jellies made from the fruit a real zing.

Mayhaws

Mayhaws are the fruit of three hawthorn species that grow from East Texas to Virginia and Florida. *Crataegus opaca* is the one most commonly found in Texas, while *C. aestivalis* and *C. rufula* occur to our east. They typically grow in swampy areas and acid soils, but they also flourish in upland orchards with irrigation and the same good management one would give any fruit crop. They are equally successful when used in the landscape as small to medium-sized flowering trees.

Early settlers soon realized they could be used to make great jellies, syrups, pies, and even wine. Unfortunately, though, they are too tart to be eaten fresh and a bit small, too. Most mayhaws run ⅜ to ¾ inch in diameter, with some selected varieties up to an inch in diameter. It's quite common to see signs for mayhaw jelly or mayhaws (in season, April/May) when one is driving along an East Texas highway.

Mayhaw trees are not commonly available in nurseries. The named varieties are even harder to find. You may have to learn how to graft or bud your own trees but the effort is worth it. Super Spur, Big Red (No. 1 Big), and T. O. Warren Superberry are some of the more popular varieties.

Mayhaw Jelly

To cook mayhaws: Combine a gallon container of mayhaws with 1 gallon of water. Cook until tender; strain through cheesecloth, making sure to get every last drop of juice. This should yield about 10 cups of juice. If not, add enough water to make 10 cups.

To make jelly: Combine 5 cups of juice with 7 cups of sugar, and use with 1 box of Sure-Jell as directed (apple or crabapple jelly would be similar).

the southern kitchen garden

Pomegranates

Pomegranates have been considered a minor fruit in the South, but there is a renewed interest in this ancient fruit, and it makes a beautiful large shrub or small tree to accent the kitchen garden. Unfortunately, many varieties tend to produce poorly in areas where there is high humidity during the growing season—the variety Wonderful is especially *not wonderful* because of limited production and poor-quality fruit. Pome-

The pomegranate has been prized since ancient times and it is currently being rediscovered. Not only is it tasty—the Cloud variety pictured is one of the sweeter ones for fresh consumption—it is good for you. Rich in antioxidants, pomegranates seem to be everywhere these days. They would make a splendid backdrop for the kitchen garden in your yard.

granates are really much better adapted to a dry, arid climate. The plants do make excellent ornamentals with the possibility of producing edible fruit. Pomegranates have seen a real increase in interest in recent years as a juice fruit with many health benefits, high in antioxidants. Trees are vigorous and free from most disease and insect problems. Most varieties will be frequently frozen out or back to the ground in the upper South.

POMEGRANATE VARIETIES

Variety	Remarks/Description
Ambrosia	Fantastically huge fruits: up to three times the size of Wonderful. Pale pink skin, purple sweet-tart juice, similar to Wonderful. Long lived, any soil. Inland or coastal climate. Self-fruitful. Very early so it may be damaged by late spring frosts.
Cloud	White fleshed and sweet for fresh consumption. Good producer.
Eversweet	Very sweet, virtually seedless fruit. Red skin, clear (nonstaining) juice. Harvest late summer through fall. Coast or inland. Grow as an 8- to 10-foot arching shrub, or train as tree or espalier. Large, showy, orange-red flowers. Self-fruitful.
Fleishman	Large, rounded fruit, about 3 inches in diameter, pink outside and inside. Very sweet flavor, seeds relatively soft, quality very good. Cold sensitive.
Purple	Very dark fruit—almost black. Very ornamental with sweet fruits.
Sweet (syn. Sweet Spanish)	Sweeter fruit than Wonderful, more widely adapted (better quality in cool-summer climates). Small, glossy-leafed, ornamental tree with showy orange-red blossoms in late spring. Suitable to espalier and container growing. Self-fruitful.

Jujubes

Jujubes can be grown virtually anywhere in the South. Most fruit crops require a certain amount of spraying if the fruit is to be free of disease and insect blemishes. Then you have to fight the birds, raccoons, and other varmints for the fruit. Jujubes might just be the exception. Birds and two-legged varmints do seem to find them some years, but otherwise they seem to be a fruit you really can grow organically.

If they're this easy, then there must be something wrong with them, right? The early varieties introduced into this country a hundred years ago tended to be very thorny with small, sour fruits. Newer varieties are sweet as candy with a nice blend of tartness, and some varieties are almost as large as a plum. The skins are still a bit tough but not objectionable, and the fruits ripen late in the season—July/September when fresh fruit is

Jujubes are virtually pest free so this is one fruit you can grow organically without spraying even a few organic pesticides. Think of them as a small crisp apple that ripens in late summer or fall when fresh fruit is hard to come by. Cook them in a heavy syrup and you have an excellent date substitute.

scarce. Think of them as small apples that are really good for you. In fact, jujubes are elements in a number of Asian medicinal products (jujube tea, etc.). They can also be candied to make an excellent date substitute. This product is often available in Asian grocery stores as Chinese dates or red dates.

The trees grow 25 to 30 feet tall (15–20 feet with pruning) and tend to spread by underground suckers. It's hard to find named variety jujube trees—Li and Lang are the most common. If you do find them, they are probably grafted. This means the suckers that pop up will be rootstock with small, sour fruits. The Meyer's Nursery in California (see Resources) is a major source for new varieties. Most varieties have thorns, but a few are relatively thornless. The foliage is a beautiful, glossy green, and the tiny yellow flowers are very fragrant. They should be easy to blend into the landscape without establishing a separate fruit orchard.

Variety	Ripe/Color	Remarks/Description
GA866	Brown	Large, elongated fruit, sugars near 45%, poor production, August
GI7-62	Reddish brown and yellow stripes	Round, flattened fruit, very sweet, August
Lang	Half-brown	Large, pear-shaped fruit, best half brown, very productive, fair quality; use for dehydration or jujube butter, late
Li	Yellow-green	Large, round fruit, good quality and best when yellow-green in mid-August
Shui Men (Sui Men)	Best after developing some brown skin color	Large, elongated fruit produced on a vigorous tree
So	Brown	Tree with zig-zag growth habit, round, sweet, August
Sugar Cane	Brown	Small to medium size, very sweet, crunchy, August
Sweet Meaty	Brown	Extremely vigorous, thorny and productive, sweet tart, marble sized
Tsao	Brown	Fruit pointed at both ends, sweet fruit, early August

Bananas and Other Weird Fruits

The quest for exotic fruit makes normally sane gardeners plant some really bizarre plants. Then they use extreme methods just to prove they can succeed at something they should never have tried. Usually these gardeners have scored with petunias, tomatoes, and the normal fruits like pears. They need a challenge, a mountain to climb. Sometimes they are just stubborn; a few may even be stupid. Most are running on a full tank of ignorance—at least at the start—and much to the chagrin of plant experts, they often succeed.

The quest might be as simple as planting an avocado seed from the grocery store or as complicated as plant exploration in another country. You can never underestimate their sincerity. Early in my career as an extension agent (Adams) I was asked by a gentleman about growing bananas in Houston. Chuckling, I pointed out, "Bananas grow well in Panama. Why don't you move to Panama and take your bananas with you?" He failed to share my humor and called a bunch of people (bosses) who could directly impact my future. Needless to say, I learned a lot about bananas in the next few weeks. I've also eaten a bunch (pun intended) of tasty, locally grown bananas since then. As long as we're having mild winters, there's a good chance folks will harvest bananas in the fall.

The trick is to get the large fruiting trunks through the winter unharmed. Some people wrap them with layers of newspaper, then white paper and red ribbons for Christmas decorations. Others use aluminum-coated insulation normally reserved for ductwork, making them look like alien rocket ships. Mulching will help, and planting on the south side of the house isn't a bad idea, either. If all goes well, during the next fall watch the bananas to see when the ridges on the fruit begin to round off. They can be harvested at this stage and allowed to ripen in the garage, or as long as temperatures stay above freezing, leave them on the plant. If they stay on until they develop a yellow color, you can expect a real taste treat.

Hardy **bananas** (*hardy* is a relative term) may survive the mild winters along the upper Gulf Coast and farther south, but they don't survive a winter like the one of 1983 with a week of freezing temperatures. In the Rio Grande valley and in south Florida, they have a better chance.

Gran Nain   Comparatively dwarf with large fruit clusters

Pysang Raja   Tall, hardy variety, delicious pinkish fruit

Rajapuri   Tough and hardy with medium-size fruit

Avocados are rarely successful even in the Rio Grande valley, but if you want to try them, look for Mexican avocados. Most commercial varieties are West Indian (the giant ones from Florida), Guatemalan, or hybrids of Mexican and Guatemalan types. The Mexican types have fruit with a thin skin and a large seed in relation to the fruit size. The foliage also has an anise fragrance when crushed. Adding to the confusion, avocados are classified as type A or type B. One sheds pollen in the morning but is receptive the next afternoon and vice versa. One of the most successful home plantings we ever saw was in South Houston where a lady had planted six seeds in one spot in the backyard. She had purchased the fruit at a stand in the valley and the trees grew up together as one plant. They were apparently Mexican avocados, and the six plants together must have solved the pollination problem.

More exotic fruits like the **star fruit** (*Averrhoa carambola*), **lychee** (*Litchi chinensis*), and **mango** (*Mangifera indica*) will require that you first build a conservatory, though most of the tropical fruits can be grown in southern Florida; some will make in the Rio Grande valley of Texas.

The **loquat** (*Eriobotrya japonica*) seems a bit confused. It blooms in the fall and the tiny fruits have to survive the winter before they can mature. In gardens from Houston south, they often do mature, but the plants will survive 100 miles or so north of this area. Loquats should be looked on as one of those gifts "nature" occasionally bestows on us following a mild winter. They ripen about the same time as strawberries, and the two, combined, make a wonderful jam. The loquat fruit is too tart to eat fresh until it begins to turn orange-ripe, and even then they contain a lot of large seeds.

The **pawpaw** (*Asimina triloba*) has a wonderful name, and the fruit isn't bad, either, though it does contain a number of large seeds. The problem is that most pawpaws are seedlings, and the fruit is rather variable. The basic flavor impression is of vanilla custard, but some fruits finish with a hint of kerosene. Even if you don't like the fruit, the trees are pretty. Pawpaws have large tropical-looking leaves and grow in a pyramidal shape to 25 feet or less. They are typically understory trees preferring a slightly acid, deep loam soil. Good drainage is essential, but they won't stand drought conditions without watering. For a plant that grows from Michigan to Florida, they aren't readily available in nurseries. Try nurseries that specialize in native plants, and ask for pawpaws grown from seed that originated in a similar climate. Michigan pawpaws wouldn't be at home in the South.

The **goumi fruit** (*Elaeagnus multiflora*) develops on a small deciduous relative of the silverberry (*Elaeagnus pungens*), a common shrub in southern landscapes. The goumi usually grows as a small tree with these bright red, metallic berries. It prefers the higher rainfall and soil acidity of the southeast gardens though it isn't commonly grown anywhere. Gardeners in Louisiana have a slightly better appreciation for this native of China. In fact, Louisiana Nursery in Opelousas, Louisiana, is one of the few mail-order sources for this plant we've seen. One of us tried making some jelly with the berries once. Nice red color, no discernable flavor. Apparently the birds like them, though.

the floral connection

Flowers feed the spirit—actually some can even feed you, as in edible flowers, but mostly they belong in the kitchen garden because of their beauty and because there is more to life than sitting down at the table. It's a commonly accepted theory that even the caveman picked wildflowers for his girlfriends to enjoy while he roasted mammoth steaks over an open fire. We're much more sophisticated these days: we include flowers in the garden because of their beauty but also because they help to attract beneficial insects—even pretty ones like butterflies that mostly benefit the soul. Granted, there are edible flowers and some like nasturtiums are quite good, but this characteristic is more of a bonus for most gardeners. We just want flowers in our gardens! Since flowers respond to the seasons, it is important to consider them just like we do vegetables—as warm or cool season varieties. Try the following in your southern kitchen garden.

WARM SEASON FLOWERS

In the kitchen garden you will mostly use annuals because just like the vegetables and many herbs the plantings will constantly be changing. Perennials (many are short lived in the South, anyway) will sometimes work and the occasional shrub or well-mannered small tree is not forbidden. An Arizona ash or live oak would obviously seem out of place and in a few years would dominate the garden as well.

Butterfly plants: Ageratums and eupatoriums, especially Gregg's Blue Mist flower, butterfly weed (*Asclepias* spp.), bouvardia, feather celosia, basketflower, coreopsis, cosmos, purple coneflower, hamelia, lantana, gayfeather, flowering tobacco, pentas, phlox, rudbeckia, marigold, tithonia, verbena, ironweed, and zinnia

Butterfly host plants: Aristolochia (Dutchman's pipe), milkweeds (*Asclepias* spp.), passiflora, fennel, dill, and parsley

Hummingbird plants: abutilon, hyssop, hollyhock, anisacanthus, cleome, hamelia, impatiens, cypress vine, morning glory, shrimp plant, jacobinia, lantana, false Turk's-cap, four-o'clock, flowering tobacco, firespike (*Odontonema*), pentas, petunia, phlox, *Salvia* spp., Texas betony (*Stachys coccinea*), yellow bells, and zinnia

COOL SEASON FLOWERS

There aren't as many cool season flowers to pick from, and they really don't bloom that much with cold weather, short days, and clouds, but many can be established in the fall for a brilliant show in the spring. The few butterflies hanging around will have to rely on dianthus and alyssum. Mostly this is a time to plant. Bulbs—especially old-fashioned daffodils like Gran Primo or Campernelle, multiflora hyacinths, Byzantine gladiolus, montbretia (crocosmia), society garlic, tigridia, lycoris, schoolhouse lily (*Rhodophiala*), leucojum, tuberose (*Polianthes tuberosa*), and rainlilies—don't take much space and they aren't very aggressive.

Also plant annuals like snapdragon, English daisy, calendula, cornflower, wallflower, larkspur, forget-me-not, foxglove, sweet pea, linaria, stock, poppy, petunia, phlox, nasturtium (frost sensitive), viola, and pansy.

THE BEST CUT FLOWERS

Almost any flower can be cut and expected to last in a bud vase through dinner, but which ones can you enjoy for several days or even weeks? Fortunately, we are blessed with a number of flowers that can be field grown; when properly cut and handled, they can be expected to last, often longer than the ones we might purchase at a floral shop.

Everlastings will obviously last a long time. Some of the best to blend in with the kitchen garden are winged everlasting (*Ammobium alatum*), cockscomb (*Celosia argentea*), feather cockscomb (*Celosia spicata*), globe amaranth (*Gomphrena globosa*), strawflower (*Helichrysum* spp.), statice (*Limonium sinensis*), love-in-a-mist (*Nigella damascena*), and starflower (*Scabiosa stellata*). The winged everlasting, cockscombs, and globe amaranth are true hot weather flowers for the summer garden the others benefit from early spring planting—even if you have to protect them from early spring frosts. In fact, statice, love-in-a-mist, and starflower will typically benefit from fall planting, especially in zone 8 and farther south. Strawflower really doesn't like hot weather and won't stand a hard freeze. Try growing large plants in 4-inch or larger pots (protected in a cold frame or greenhouse) and set them out after the last spring frost.

To keep the flowers fresh, you can place them in a vase of water for several days; then to transform them into everlastings, simply hang them upside down in bundles to dry and enjoy for years to come.

Warm season cut flowers include the everlastings like cockscomb and globe amaranth (which also look great fresh) and lots more. Sunflowers come in such a stunning array of sizes and colors you could make a career of growing sunflowers. And they make great cut flowers. Most are produced on rather large plants, including the varieties Starburst Lemon Aura, Claret, Italian White, and Soraya AAS. If you don't have room for a 5- to 6-foot flower in your garden, then look to the dwarf varieties like Double Dandy, Sundance Kid, and Sunspot. The tall-growing ageratums, coreopsis, large-flowered marigolds like Gold Coin, and zinnias like Oklahoma, Benary's Giant, and Zowie (2006 AAS) not only look great in a vase on the table, but they add interest and color to the kitchen garden. Many of them—especially the ageratums and zinnias—will also draw butterflies like a magnet.

Dahlias are just one of the many cut flowers you can grow in your garden to "feed the soul" and brighten the table. Be sure to plant the tubers early so the flowers will bloom before it gets too hot. With good drainage and raised beds dahlias often come back for years.

Cool season cut flowers aren't as numerous, but pansies and violas can be cut and displayed in a bud vase. Snapdragons flourish in the late winter/spring along with dianthus, English daisy (*Bellis perennis*), calendula, bachelor's button, larkspur, Chinese forget-me-not, foxglove, sweet pea, linaria, stock, poppies, annual phlox, German primrose, and nasturtiums. Most of these cool season flowers grow well enough in the fall/winter, but they don't bloom much until late winter/early spring. Nasturtiums and calendulas like cool weather, but they often freeze out without the protection of a cold frame or a heavy blanket when temperatures fall below 32°.

Perennial cut flowers may overlap some of the previous lists. It's important to remember that most perennials are short lived in the southern garden, anyway. But for argument's sake, the following are considered perennials. Yarrow (*Achillea millefolium*) is actually rather permanent and a great cut flower. Also expect purple coneflower (*Echinacea* spp.) to survive for a number of years. The closely related yellow coneflower (*Rudbeckia* spp.) is another short-lived version of a perennial wildflower. It is great for cutting but needs to be replanted each year like an annual. Bluebells (Lisianthus, Eustoma) are listed as perennial wildflowers, but they only last a season or two, although they tend to reseed prolifically in wildflower fields where they are adapted. Salvias, like Mexican sage (*Salvia leucantha*) and mealycup sage (*Salvia farinacea*), are prolific bloomers with long-lasting cut flowers. Garden mums are making a comeback, and a number of old-fashioned and new varieties are available such as Country Girl (pink), Clara Curtis (pink), Duchess of Edinburgh (red), and Marie Stocker (golden apricot). These hardy garden beauties are worth revisiting.

HARVESTING AND CARING FOR CUT FLOWERS

The mere basics are to cut the flowers and immediately put them in a bucket of water large enough to allow recutting the stems underwater. This eliminates air pockets in the flower stem conductive tissue and ensures that water and floral preservative (if you choose to use it) will be available to the flower. What is this mysterious floral preservative? It typically includes sugar (a food source) and an acid like citric acid to inhibit the growth of micro-organisms that could plug the conductive tissue. In combination, these materials feed the flowers and ensure that they can take up water over a reasonable period of time.

TRIMMING FLOWERING PLANTS

Even those beautiful flowering plants in your cutting garden will benefit from an occasional trimming. Most gardeners are very familiar with the term *deadheading*. Deadheading is the process of removing old spent flowers from the plant. This makes the plants more attractive but the primary reason for removing the old flowers is to short-circuit the formation of seed. The primary reason that plants flower is to produce seed. By removing old flowers before the seed develops, you greatly increase the number of flowers produced each season. The primary reason for deadheading in the garden then is to encourage the formation of additional flowers that may then be cut and brought into the home for you to enjoy. Most flowering plants go through a number of stages, and some of these stages can be unattractive. To keep the garden at its best, you may find it necessary to trim back your flowering plants during those periods when the foliage has become brown or the plants have grown excessively and are crowding other plantings that are in prime condition. Seasonal pruning is an important part of maintaining an attractive kitchen garden.

KNOT GARDENS

The knot garden found its beginnings in Tudor times, and from the knot garden the maze evolved. Early knot gardens were large, to say the least. The early Tudors filled spaces of the knot garden with a variety of materials including flowers such as carnations, vegetables like cabbage and kale, and small fruits such as strawberries, raspberries, and gooseberries. The present-day knot garden is a scaled-down version.

The basic premise of a knot garden is to create regular geometric and symmetrical patterns out of evergreen herbs, planted in continuous ribbons. The pattern ideas have been taken from such items as jewelry, embroidery, tapestry, and even nature. Designs can be adapted to fit a variety of spaces ranging from large and formal to small and intimate. As the size of the pattern decreases, so should the complexity—something as simple as a cartwheel, a circle divided into wedges, with each wedge being planted with a different contrasting herb or vegetable. The closed knot design is better suited for a small area where the pattern is solidly planted. Where space permits, the open knot, in which the areas between the ribbons are left open, can create a striking and exciting landscape feature. The open areas can be filled with materials such as bark mulch, gravel, brick, flagstone slabs, or a variety of groundcovers.

The use of a single evergreen herb can be attractive, but the use of two or three herbs with contrasting foliage or texture can create a show-stopping impact. The interwoven effect when combining different herbs can be created by stopping one line (ribbon) of plants, allowing the crossing line (ribbon) to be continuous. By allowing the crossing lines to grow a little taller than the surrounding plants, you create the illusion that they pass over the lower ribbon.

During the planning stages, it's probably best to start by putting your idea down on paper. You can then take your ideas and transfer them to the planting area. This can be done by laying out a grid using stakes and string. The center of the square can be located by running string diagonally from the four corners. You can easily create a circle or semicircle by driving a stake in the center and using a string tied to the center stake and some marking paint or pouring sand out of a

the floral connection

bottle to create your arches or circle. Once the pattern has been laid out on the ground, you can begin planting your plants. The spacing should be based on the size of the plants when they are mature. You want the plants to be close enough to fill in quickly but not so close that they become overcrowded.

Once you've planted the knot garden, you should begin manicuring the plants to create the visual appearance you desire. Remember to trim the plants so the crown is narrower than the base. This allows light to reach the lower limbs and helps to prevent excessive thinning of the foliage on the lower branches. Knot gardens are not a low-maintenance endeavor. You will need to trim your knot garden regularly to keep it neat and attractive.

SIX

soil preparation and garden management

Soil is the most important element in your kitchen garden! Lousy soil, lousy garden—it's that simple. Organic matter, preferably compost, is the key to this good soil. While we agree that the judicious use of soluble fertilizers (call them chemical fertilizers, if you must) is a viable option to ensure optimum growth, if you work hard enough at enriching your soil with compost, you may never find them necessary. If you garden aggressively, then your philosophy must be "the gardener with the most compost wins." Sure, you can fail by planting the wrong varieties at the wrong time or locating your garden in too much shade, but we're presuming that you are reading this book in its entirety and you've already dealt with those basics. Now we're talking "planted in your brain, obsessive compulsion to locate and secure organic matter." If you can't get compost, go for wood chips and use them only as mulch. Eventually you will get them to break down so they can be added to the soil. Check out the local stable, or buy a load of mushroom compost. The yearly, even seasonal addition of organic matter is not an option; it's a necessity.

TO AMEND OR START FROM SCRATCH?

Almost regardless of the "soil hand" you're dealt, you can amend it to be a productive soil. The question you have to ask is, Is it worth it? Clay soils are difficult to work with, but they have the potential to hold nutrients and water if they are amended with enough organic matter. At times even a clay soil with lots of organic matter can hold too much water. Work the planting beds up into ridges, then plant on top of the ridge, and to some extent you've solved the drainage problem.

An alternative to raised beds is to work the soil into ridges and plant on the ridge. Even a clay soil in a high rainfall area can be counted on to produce a bountiful harvest with this treatment. Make sure you also add a generous amount of compost to the soil each year.

Sandy soils are easy to work, but water and fertilizer elements leach rapidly through them. Again organic matter is the key. Mixing 4 to 6 inches of compost with a sandy soil prior to planting will make a tremendous difference. Sandy soils also are a haven for gophers and microscopic roundworms called *nematodes*. Gophers tunnel through the soil munching on your favorite veggies—wait until you see a wilting broccoli plant pulled halfway into a hole. You'll hate gophers and wonder if that nice sand is so great after all. Nematodes attack the root system of favorite crops like okra and tomatoes causing them to be stunted, nutrient deficient, and even wilted. More compost can help to reduce nematode populations by encouraging beneficial micro-organisms, but it won't do much to slow down gophers. The gophers will need to be exterminated—and they are quick to repopulate.

Raised beds are the answer for most of us, and they work especially well in a kitchen garden. You can use all sorts of building materials to construct the beds—2 × 12 boards work fine, or you can use rock, broken concrete (and score a few environmental points), railroad ties, and so forth. Worried about the toxic materials used to treat railroad ties? Don't eat the ties, and you should be fine. Very little is leached into the soil, and plants don't pick it up.

The soil mix you put into the beds is critical. Most "dirt yards" have some sort of soil mix—usually consisting of one part organic matter (compost, if you're lucky, but usually bark or wood chips if you're not), one part top soil, and one part aggregate (coarse sand, perlite, haydite, etc.). They typically don't add any mineral nutri-

the southern kitchen garden

This is the Adams kitchen garden during construction with 2 x 12 raised beds and irrigation lines in place. After lots of leveling and a generous amount of compost-rich soil the garden absolutely erupts with vegetables, herbs, and flowers during every season of the year.

tion so mixing some fertilizer (2–4 pounds of 15-5-10 or 13-13-13 per 100 square feet of bed area) plus some micronutrients and an organic fertilizer like cottonseed meal (10 pounds per 100 square feet) prior to planting is advisable. You may still find that you have to foliar feed on a regular basis to promote rapid growth when you are working with your first crops in a new bed. Also expect that organic matter will oxidize (burn up slowly) and that your soil level will sink. Just keep adding organic matter like mushroom compost and soluble fertilizers as needed and the garden should remain productive indefinitely. Every 2 to 3 years it's a good idea to have the Cooperative Extension Service test your soil to make sure the pH isn't out of line (pH 6.0–7.0 is best for most vegetables) and to check on soil nutrients. Don't be surprised if they recommend cutting back on nitrogen—it's not a very accurate test, and they're used to testing field soils. If your garden is healthy and productive, continue to side-dress or foliar feed to promote rapid growth.

Keep an eye on your phosphorus level as well. Phosphorus doesn't leach readily from the soil. Years and years of using fertilizers high in phosphorus can create some serious imbalances. Plants do need phosphorus, and it is an important nutrient in plant growth, but overuse can be just as disastrous. Excessively high levels of phosphorus can cause nitrogen and iron to become tied up to the point that they are almost unavailable to your garden plants. About the only way to overcome excessive phosphorus is to stop using any fertilizer containing phosphorus and allow enough time to pass to deplete what you already have. This can be particularly difficult for

Compost pile showing the layering of leaves, soil, and grass clippings. Turning the pile every two weeks can speed up the process. Be sure to water—especially at first and during dry periods and include manure or other nitrogen sources to feed the hungry microbes.

the organic gardener because most organic fertilizers will contain at least some level of phosphorus. The best way to avoid this problem is to keep an eye on it, be aware that the problem exists, and avoid overusing high-phosphorus fertilizers. If the problem does occur, you may be able to use foliar feeding to supply iron and other elements that are tied up in the soil.

MULCHING

Mulch is indispensable in the kitchen garden. It not only keeps down weeds and conserves moisture, it keeps the soil cooler in the summer and organic mulches decompose to add more organic matter to the soil. In the winter you can even pull up mulch around the base of plants to get some frost protection. Not all mulches are the same (see "Physiological Disorders" and the prairie hay mulch from hell). You can use some materials like wood chips or pine needles that wouldn't be good soil additives because they are too high in carbon and too low in nitrogen as a mulch, but you may have to rake them off rather than incorporating them into the soil at the end of the season. Store them in a pile each off-season until they are thoroughly decomposed. Hint: A few cups of a complete fertilizer each year while these materials are in storage will speed up the process. Of course, you can also be somewhat cavalier about sprinkling fertilizer on the mulch between the rows during the growing season since it has something of a sponge ef-

the southern kitchen garden

Material	Approximate Pounds/100 Pounds of Fertilizer or Percentage			
	Nitrogen (N)	Phosphorus ($0P_2O_5$)	Potassium (K_2O)	Quantity (Pounds) Needed to Supply 0.2 Pound N per 100 Square Feet
Ammonium nitrate	33.5	—	—	½
Ammonium sulfate	21.0	—	—	1
Calcium nitrate	15.5	—	—	1½
Potassium nitrate	13.0	—	44.0	1½
Urea	46.0	—	—	⅓
Urea formaldehyde	38.0	—	—	½
Superphosphate	—	18.0–20.0	—	N/A
Concentrated superphosphate	—	45.0–46.0	—	N/A
Potassium chloride	—	—	60.0–62.0	N/A
Potassium sulfate	—	—	50.0–53.0	N/A
13-13-13	13.0	13.0	13.0	1½
12-24-12	12.0	24.0	12.0	1½
15-5-10	15.0	5.0	10.0	1¼

fect to keep the fertilizer from immediately being available in the soil below. Using a layer of newspapers 8 to 10 sheets thick under the organic mulch is another way of constructing a barrier to weeds and slowing down the movement of fertilizer elements into the root zone. Usually by the end of the season the newspaper, at least, will be ready for incorporation.

Plastic or other synthetic mulches may find their way into your kitchen garden. Black plastic is a bit ugly and mostly unnecessary, but red plastic mulch or reflective mulches may prove interesting for their insect repellent qualities.

IRRIGATION

Next to soil management, there isn't much that is more important than supplying your garden with good water at the proper time. While there are a number of ways to irrigate, low-volume systems like drip or microsprinkler are the most efficient way to apply water. Leaky tubing is another low-volume system that works well in the kitchen garden. If these systems are set up with a time clock, you can almost forget the time-consuming drudgery of watering. Of course it's good therapy to water the garden by hand occasionally, and the "hands-on" approach is best when you're planting seed or setting out transplants.

It is most efficient to utilize water during periods of low temperature and light winds. Unfortunately, this means watering after dark, and as a general rule, it is not recommended to water at night. The longer the foliage remains wet, the more

Material	Approximate Pounds/100 Pounds of Fertilizer or Percentage			
	Nitrogen (N)	Phosphorus (P_2O_5)	Potassium (K_2O)	Quantity (Pounds) Needed to Supply 0.2 Pound N per 100 Square Feet
Alfalfa hay	0.025	Trace	0.025	800
Bat guano	10.0	4.0	2.0	2
Bonemeal	1.0	15.0	—	10
Cottonseed meal	6.0	3.0	1.5	3
Fish meal	10.0	6.0	—	2
Kelp	1.0	0.5	9.0	20
Manures (dried)				
Chicken	3.0	5.0	1.5	7
Cow	1.5	2.0	2.3	14
Horse	2.1	1.0	2.3	10
Pig	2.1	0.4	0.5	10
Sheep	4.2	2.5	6.0	5
Manures (fresh)				
Chicken	1.5	1.0	0.5	14
Cow	0.5	0.2	0.5	40
Horse	0.7	0.3	0.5	30
Pig	0.7	0.6	0.7	30
Sheep	1.4	0.7	1.5	15
Soybean hay	0.025	Trace	Trace	800
Used mushroom compost	1.0	1.0	1.0	20

likely it is that you will have disease problems. In order to reduce loss of water caused by evaporation and wind, try watering very early in the morning, even just prior to sunup, or at least use a drip system that doesn't get the foliage wet.

PLANT PROTECTION FROM FROST AND THE ELEMENTS

At any season of the year, nature's forces can threaten your kitchen garden. In the fall, winter, and early spring we worry about frost or a hard freeze damaging our tender plants. Virtually year-round dry, blowing winds are a force that is over-looked, but this is a weather element that can be almost as devastating to your garden as the temperature—quickly drying out and abrading tissues that may be too tender to survive. In the summer the sun becomes too intense, the rains are too infrequent, and the wind continues to blow. There are days when you wonder why you even try to grow a garden (that's why gardeners have other hobbies like photography, fishing, or hunting).

Barbara Ferer's garden with raised beds, rich with compost, and topped with a low-volume irrigation system to promote rapid growth. The onions are just getting started while bamboo poles wait along the fence to stake the tomatoes and peppers that will be planted later.

The development of fiber row cover for use in the garden is one of the most significant new techniques gardeners have at their disposal in the twenty-first century. The idea really isn't new—the cloche (a glass bell jar) precedes this product (a spin-off of diaper liner technology) by centuries. However, row cover is cheap compared with the glass cloche and is easy to use. The main benefit of using row

Frost blanket, enhanced with a blanket of snow, protects tender cool season vegetables during a rare cold snap at the Harris County Extension (Houston, Texas) test gardens. Some cool season veggies like onions and cabbage are "tough as nails" while others like broccoli and cauliflower can be damaged especially in the heading stage.

Fiber row cover makes a great wrap for tomato cages in the early spring. It only provides a small amount of frost protection, but it protects the plants from drying wind and it can serve to exclude insects. Use clothespins to fasten it and when the plants are knee high remove the covers and store them for use next year.

cover is to protect tender transplants from the drying effects of the wind. It may also help to keep out insects early in the development of a crop, and it even provides a small amount of frost protection. Its thicker brother "frost blanket" does an even better job in this respect.

How do you use these miracle products? There are several ways to apply them. The simplest is to drape the material over the row and weight it down with boards, rocks, and the like, around the sides of the bed. Leave it loose, and most plants will grow and push it up. If you want to support it, use plastic irrigation tubing hoops over the row. The other way to use these materials is around wire tomato cages. Wrap the material around the cage leaving extra at the top; then secure it with clothespins. After the tomatoes or peppers are knee high, remove the row cover and store it for another season.

Lots of other plant protection devices are available, from miniature greenhouses to plant protectors constructed with tube compartments that are designed to hold water and serve as mini–solar collectors. In a pinch, most gardeners pack some hay or mulch around the tender plants and wrap or cover them with an old blanket or other good insulator. A single layer of clear plastic can be used to block the wind, but it needs to be placed outside the insulation. If you only use the single layer of plastic it can be colder under the cover than the outside temperature. This depends on the duration of the cold spell—and you do get wind protection—but a single layer just doesn't have any insulation value.

the southern kitchen garden

SEVEN

pests

Insects, diseases, weeds, and even varmints can wreck your best intentions when it comes to gardening. Don't put up with it—fight back! The kitchen garden usually isn't large enough to share. Maybe you've heard someone say, "I just plant extra so the bugs can have some." We don't care to eat after bugs; and, honestly, the bugs usually take all of it or at least sample it all. Diseases can be just as bad. Unlike with insects, you can't wait until the disease reaches some threshold level, as it may be too late to save the crop. For example, if you wait until half of the tomato foliage has turned brown from early blight, an application of fungicide won't do much to save the crop because too many of the leaves necessary for photosynthesis have been lost. Even if the plant produces new leaves, with the onset of high temperatures, you will get very little fruit set. Usually with a disease problem, we anticipate it (as in early blight of tomatoes) and spray to prevent it. Weeds aren't a big problem in the kitchen garden because of the intensive management that this garden demands—see a weed, pull it. It's that simple.

INSECTS

Insects are only a problem when they begin to affect the quality of your garden produce. A few aphids may not seem like much to worry about, but they soon turn into hundreds, even thousands. With a small, intensively managed garden, it is easy to spot these pests early, and in most cases they can be controlled with management practices or low-toxicity sprays. Aphids (plant lice) are easy to hose off the plants with a spray of high-pressure water. Be sure to spray under the leaves. They won't walk back up on the plant, but be aware that fire ants may be farming (and protecting) them, so they may carry a few back into the plant. In some cases, the best you can do is to control ants around the garden, not in it. If you have to spray or dust, always try to use the least toxic spray materials first. Spinosad is a new organic pesticide available as a bait that can be used to control

Grasshoppers seem to be especially troublesome in the country garden. They eat everything from tomatoes to the tender shoots of fruit trees. Put out semaspore bait as soon as you see the first small "hoppers."

ants in the garden and orchard. Typically it requires more work to control pests organically because you have to treat more often to get the same effect.

Stinkbugs, especially the leaf-footed stinkbug, can be very hard to control. Even when they drop off of the plant after being sprayed with an insecticide, it is tempting to walk around and step on them to ensure that they don't get up and go back to the plant. This pest, along with a relative (the green stinkbug), sucks the juices out of plants—usually from the fruiting parts like tomatoes, southern peas, and even fruit crops. This causes the cells to die leaving corky and not too palatable areas under the skin.

Leaf-feeding beetles like the flea beetle, yellow-margined, and potato beetles can decimate the foliage of beans, potatoes, and leafy vegetables. The larval stage is often even more devastating. Early detection and spraying with a pesticide is your best bet. If you wait too late, the damage may be more severe than would justify the effort to spray, and the harvest interval (before you can harvest again after spraying) may be long enough that the beetles come back and severely damage the new growth.

The imported fire ant is a regular pest in southern gardens. Most baits and pesticides labeled for ant control aren't labeled for the garden. You can still use these products outside the garden but in the garden stick with organic products that use diatomaceous earth or spinosad.

Grasshoppers aren't much of a problem in the city but are unrelenting in the country. Low-toxicity baits that make the grasshoppers sicken and die help to slow them down if you apply the materials early in the spring. By summer, however, the hoppers have grown large, and it is hard to stop them. It is also critical to obtain fresh bait each season as these materials have a comparatively limited shelf life. Pesticides will give some control, but it is best to treat while the grasshoppers are still small. A flock of guineas may be the ultimate answer if your subdivision bylaws will allow it. Garden spiders get a few but the big grasshoppers just hop out of the web unless you remove their legs. For most folks, this process is just too slow and icky. It may help to feed a few hoppers to the spiders this way early in the season, though, just to get the spiders on track.

DISEASES

Diseases aren't a big problem in the kitchen garden; just be sure to plant disease-resistant varieties when available. Tomatoes, for example, are such an important crop that plant breeders have found resistance to a number of tomato diseases like early blight, fusarium wilt, and nematodes (microscopic roundworms that are usually covered under plant pathology). In many cases, a favorite variety doesn't have the resistance that you would like to have so you plant it anyway and deal with the consequences using cultural techniques and a minimum of sprays. For example, a cultural technique that significantly reduces disease infection is wider spacing to allow for better air circulation. Training plants to grow vertically on a trellis is another way to improve air circulation and, at the same time, make better use of limited space. More open spacing helps to keep the foliage dryer and spares some plants from the spread of disease spores because they are further apart. In the case of vertical gardening, you are getting the plants further from the soil and the previous season's diseases that can be splashed up onto the foliage. Squash fruit rot is a black, whiskery fungal growth that starts at the end of the fruit shortly after pollination. Typically the day after the bloom shrivels on the female flowers, it can easily be pulled off, which allows the end of the fruit to dry and harden more quickly. As a result, there is less infection—not a practical thing to do in a 40-acre field, but an easy chore for the kitchen gardener.

Enriching the soil with compost can reduce nematode infestation by promoting micro-organisms that attack the nematodes before they can enter the root cells. At the same time, compost and a balanced availability of nutrients encourages healthy plant growth, which is more resistant to diseases.

If you have to spray, try the low-toxicity fungicides like wettable sulfur, baking soda, or neem oil. Also anticipate special problems like early blight on tomatoes. Early season sprays with commercial fungicides usually won't be needed later on as the fruit begins to ripen, so it is easy to observe the recommended harvest waiting period (number of days after spraying before you can harvest).

Some diseases like brown rot on peaches, nectarines, and plums are so pervasive that it is virtually impossible to grow quality fruit without the use of preventative fungicide sprays. Contact your local Cooperative Extension Office for a spray schedule, and use cultural techniques like picking up and trashing any fruit that succumbs to this disease. If you don't follow good sanitation procedures, you will be allowing next year's disease inoculum to remain, and the situation becomes worse every year.

Should you find room for a pecan tree, then pecan scab is the main disease threat. Choose the most disease-resistant varieties, and avoid spraying as much as possible. Early spring applications of zinc sprays are very beneficial for the tree's nutrition, but even these materials can be staining if allowed to drift to a neighbor's property. Unfortunately, by the time you grow a pecan tree large enough to produce a good crop, you will have to pump spray materials 50 to 100 feet in the air, and there's no way to avoid spray drift. Unless you live on acreage, a pecan tree is likely to be a source more of frustration than of pecan pies.

WEEDS

Weeds are even less of a problem than insects and diseases in most kitchen gardens since the gardens are comparatively small and intensively managed. Every time you go out to plant, fertilize, harvest, or just enjoy the garden, pull a few weeds. At the end of each season, you may have to devote some special time to weeding and cleanup, but it shouldn't be too difficult. A lot may depend on the soil mix you use. For example, mushroom compost, despite being high in salts when it is fresh from the farm, is relatively free of weeds. After a little time and leaching (cleansing the soil with rainfall and irrigation water), you have a richly organic soil substrate that is easy to manage. Nut grass (purple nutsedge) is the insidious weed that most of us fear in our gardens. Don't let it get the upper hand—start early to pull out the nutsedge, making sure to try and get the nutlets in the soil, if possible. Assuming that you have a friable, organic soil, this should be easy. The true grasses can be a problem too. Seeds can blow in or aggressive creepers like Bermuda grass or Bahia grass can find their way into the beds. Blowing seeds are just a fact of life, but you may be able to keep out the runners of perennial grasses by placing a barrier of tin roofing, tar paper, and the like 18 to 24 inches deep in the soil around the garden to prevent these weedy grasses from getting a hold.

VARMINTS

Varmints might seem to be more of an annoyance than a serious problem, but tell that to someone fighting a family of gophers as they watch their broccoli plants being pulled underground or someone dealing with rats that gnaw the bottom half out of the tomatoes. Think Mr. Rabbit will only go after the greens that no one wants to eat anyway? Wrong—rabbits will eat off at ground level the onion transplants you spent all afternoon setting out, then do the same to your small broccoli and lettuce transplants. Raccoons and opossums just love fresh fruit, as do squirrels (we refer to them as "tree rats").

Gardeners often become bird-watchers—they watch them peck holes in fruit just as it begins to ripen. And it's especially frustrating because there is not much that you can do about it. While a 12-gauge shotgun might solve some of these problems in the country, city dwellers really are hand tied. Even country folk shouldn't shoot protected songbirds that have developed a taste for fresh peaches. In most instances you are forced to barricade the precious "fruits of your labor" behind fences or under the protection of plastic netting.

You can try scaring them off with plastic owls, wild-looking beach balls, or flashy tape, but birds and most other varmints are quick learners, and unless you are constantly moving the devices, they are likely to perch and poop on your plastic owl. The gardener who thought of the scarecrow wasn't into yard art. He or she was trying to scare crows away.

First you need to fence the garden if at all possible. Rabbits, leg-hiking dogs, and other animals need to be kept out of the garden. The neighbor's cat is a more difficult problem. Fences just don't work. Try one of the motion sensitive irrigation valves that releases a brief spray of water. The neighborhood cats may decide to prowl elsewhere. The fence won't suffice for all varmints. Sometimes a low-voltage electric wire will be needed to keep out the most aggressive species. Bird

Chickens in the Garden

Chickens and guineas can be an asset in the garden, but mostly they can be a nuisance. The majority of city gardeners can forget about relying on a bit of "poultry assistance" with the weeding and bug control chores. Chances are the city or subdivision won't allow it. Sometimes you can have a few "hens only," but you still have to exercise some management decisions. Feathered workers don't know weeds from lettuce seedlings; thus, you will need to control their movement until desirable garden plants are of sufficient size to survive their scratching and pecking.

If you have a fenced garden, it should be relatively easy to open the gate and allow access as conditions warrant—lots of weeds and bugs, no tender seedlings. Guineas may be harder to restrict, but they are mostly after bugs anyway. You also have to provide a coop for nighttime protection/egg laying and, if you're in the country, you will lose a few chickens to hawks and coyotes. Plan on feeding some grain to your flock, but your bonus will be eggs with really dark orange yolks.

netting works, but don't put it on until the fruit is beginning to ripen; otherwise, the tree will grow through it, and you will wish you had settled for store-bought fruit. Use some of the scare devices. It will give you something to do and the neighbors something to talk about. In the country you might try explosive noise-making devices, but they are loud and annoying to gardeners as well as to varmints.

Deer are a special problem. They can leap most garden fences in a single bound. You will have to include electric wires or install one of the special deer fences—either tall (8-plus feet) or with a sloping angle that frustrates the deer. Repellants theoretically work, but the rain soon washes them away, and the deer may get used to the hair bags you make up from the local barber shop. During hunting season, you can put a few in the freezer unless you have subdivision restrictions.

LOW-TOXICITY PEST CONTROL

Call it "organic" if you want—the truth is, most of us strive to use the least toxic pest controls that will get the job done, but we probably wouldn't pass muster if we had to conform to the more stringent tests required for someone applying for organic certification. Maybe we use some mushroom compost—it's had chemical nutrients (salts) added to enrich it or we spray a little glyphosate to kill out the Bermuda grass before we prepare the soil. Chances are we've used a hose-on fertilizer sprayer or a dose of encapsulated fertilizer pellets on the garden or pot plants. Facing the loss of a crop, we may even resort to spraying with low-toxicity commercial pesticides, but mostly we use Bt (*Bacillus thuringiensis*) to get the caterpillars; spinosad, a botanical (fungus-produced toxin) that works on a wide range of chewing pests (spinosad is also formulated as a fire ant bait); wettable sulfur for spider mites; and botanical sprays made from plant oils like neem oil or just high-pressure water sprays to get the job done. It's easier to control pests in the kitchen

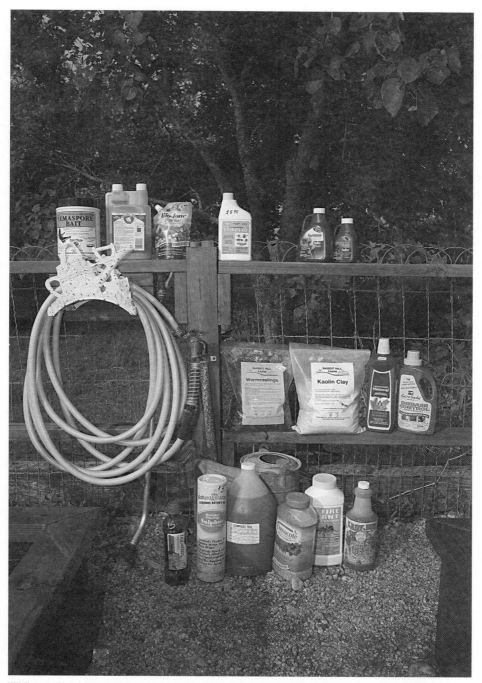

While at first glance this appears to be a purely organic arsenal of pesticides and fertilizers, it does include a soluble fertilizer and a slow-release encapsulated fertilizer. The authors' philosophy is to use tons of organic matter and if pests get out of hand, the lowest toxicity pesticide is always tried first. A judicious amount of soluble fertilizer is used and when a crop is worth saving (the pests haven't done too much damage) the gardener wins, even if it requires a commercial pesticide that is labeled for use on the crop.

pests

garden because it is close to the house, small enough to keep an eye on, and if the pests get too bad, we can pull up the affected crop and start over.

PHYSIOLOGICAL DISORDERS

This very scientific-sounding term covers maladies like nutrient stress, failure to water in newly transplanted seedlings, poor drainage or too much water, and damage from toxins like herbicides and blossom end rot. At least initially, there is no organism involved though stress can predispose the plant to infections.

Nutrient stress would seem to be an obvious problem that the average plant-sensitive gardener would recognize, but even master gardeners sometimes look at the pale green or yellow-streaked plants in test plots and wonder what is wrong. Granted, nutrient stress isn't always the culprit, but if the plants are puny and stunted following the application of a high-carbon organic matter source like wood chips, or if it's a new soil with little added nutrients and you haven't added any fertilizer—wake up, the plants are hungry! The nutrients can be supplied with organic sources like fish emulsion, or you can use a soluble fertilizer like 20-20-20. The nutrients enter the plant in the same ionic form regardless. You have to be careful with soluble fertilizers—they're salts and they can certainly burn plants if you overdo it. This is one reason the hose-on fertilizer sprayers are so handy in the small kitchen garden. You dump the bag of fertilizer into the plastic jar, add water, hook it up to the hose, and spray away. The spray is metered from the saturated solution at the top of the jar and comes out at a reduced rate just right for foliar applications. When all of the nutrients have dissolved, the color of the dye becomes pale, and you will notice that there aren't any solids left in the bottom of the jar. Add more soluble fertilizer and continue spraying. There's little chance of burning the plants, though in the summer it might be best to spray in the morning before it gets too hot.

You would think that it is obvious how important it is to water in small trans-plants after they are set out in the garden, but we've seen avid gardeners spend all morning setting transplants and then walk away as if Mother Nature were following behind with a watering can. Really you should water in these plants after you set each row or every 15 to 30 minutes depending on the time of year and whether it is really hot and dry. In late summer, it's not a bad idea to have someone follow along and water in the plants as you set them and then cover the row with fiber row cover to protect them further from the sun and wind. Let's face it: the plants are under stress—the roots may have been damaged, the sun intensity may be greater (compared with the greenhouse), and the drying effect of the wind is almost always more severe.

Watering too frequently or poor drainage—usually aggravated by tropical rains—can take out your garden in a matter of days. When the pore spaces in the soil become saturated with water, there isn't enough oxygen for the roots to function properly, and the plants wilt and often die. The symptoms are essentially like drought stress because the plants can't take up the water that is there. The solution is to monitor the amount of irrigation water you apply carefully, plant in raised beds, or work the soil up into ridges with plants on the ridge and provide for additional drainage, if necessary, with underground tile drainage or surface ditches.

Herbicides usually aren't a problem in a kitchen garden, but because so many of our favorite vegetables are ultrasensitive to these chemicals, sometimes they sneak up on us. Glyphosate and similar "kill through the foliage but don't hurt the soil" products are tempting to use in the garden. We rarely need them in the kitchen garden because we can pull most of the weeds. But suppose you let a bed lay fallow for a few seasons, and the weeds have gotten the upper hand. You might be tempted to spray the bed with glyphosate to kill the perennial weeds like Bermuda grass so you can get off to a good start the next season. Tomatoes are very sensitive to this chemical and seem to always be in the way of a little spray drift. If you see bleached areas in the foliage, suspect you got a little close with the glyphosate. Technically, you can't use it in a producing garden, but you can use it to prepare for the next season. Most kitchen gardeners will never find a use for it at all.

Sometimes the herbicide comes from an unexpected source and as a result of your best intentions. One year in our Extension Test Garden, we noticed that the tomatoes in several rows appeared to have symptoms of a virus infection. One row with prairie grass hay used for mulch was especially bad. The foliage was distorted with shoestringlike tips on the leaves and the foliage was also chlorotic with interveinal yellowing. Other rows had intermediate symptoms where we had used alfalfa hay for mulch. The plant pathologists at Texas A&M University determined that the culprit was picloram, an herbicide used in hay fields to eliminate broad-leaved weeds. Enough was present in the prairie grass hay to leach into the soil and affect the tomato plants. The plants with alfalfa mulch (picloram could not be used on this broad-leaved hay crop) should have been symptom free. So what happened? We had used some of the prairie grass hay to pack around the plants for frost protection and enough remained to produce intermediate symptoms. Our pathologists explained that uniform symptoms usually mean herbicide damage while virus infections typically begin as spotted infections in the garden.

Blossom end rot is essentially caused by water stress. The distal end of the fruit—usually tomatoes are the crop of concern—doesn't get enough water, and the cells begin to die. A dark spot begins to show up at the blossom end of the fruit and it eventually widens to a dark, water-soaked area. Initially disease organisms are not involved, but the damaged tissue may ultimately become infected with a decay organism. It may sound strange, but too much water can cause this problem as can too little water. It is especially critical during fruit production and as the stress of summer weather begins to factor in. Tomatoes growing in a container are especially vulnerable because of the rapid drainage, limited root system, and the potential for water stress. Even in a large 30-gallon pot, the plant may need to be watered several times per day to supply the water necessary for a plant with a heavy fruit set to mature the fruit successfully. In the garden setting, heavy rains and a clay soil can cause

Blossom end rot is caused by a lack of water to the developing end of the fruit. Dry weather can cause it or stressing a container-grown plant for water can start the process. Too much water can also be the culprit since plants in a waterlogged soil can't take up water. Plant in raised beds or on ridges and use mulch to conserve moisture during dry spells. Water container-grown tomatoes twice a day when they are laden with fruit—even if you have to use an irrigation system with a timer. Calcium sprays can also help.

similar problems because the soil becomes waterlogged; and without enough oxygen in the soil, the roots can't function efficiently to take up water. It's also important to keep the soil evenly moist. Periods of water stress followed by too much water—and more water stress—are a sure formula for blossom end rot (BER). To reduce the incidence of BER, plant in raised beds or on ridges in the garden, use a low-volume irrigation system to keep the rows evenly watered, use a mulch to conserve moisture, and consider using a calcium supplement if BER has been a persistent problem. Plants with an adequate supply of available calcium are less susceptible to BER. In a sandy, acid soil (which might include raised beds even though the subsoil is alkaline), liming the soil based on a soil test recommendation may do the trick. Calcium chloride salt solutions are available for foliar treatment, and calcium nitrate fertilizer can be used to side-dress the beds with both nitrogen and a soluble form of calcium. Most soils contain lots of calcium, but often it is not readily available to the plant.

the southern kitchen garden

becoming a successful plant propagator

As you become more involved in the field of gardening, you may find that the limited variety of plants available to you at area nurseries and garden centers is not enough to satisfy your desires. It may become necessary for you to take your gardening activities a step further into the world of plant propagation. Plant propagation is a field of study in horticulture or gardening where you learn the techniques needed to start and multiply the plants in and around your garden.

Most common garden plants can easily be started from seed, cuttings, division, layering, and even budding and grafting. By following a few simple steps, almost anyone can become an accomplished plant propagator.

STARTING WITH SEED

Seeds are where the life of the garden begins. To become an accomplished kitchen gardener, you will need to master the skills necessary to start plants from seed. Whether you're growing transplants to plant in the garden or planting seed directly, there are a few things you will need to know to be successful.

It is important to remember that seeds are living organisms. Although they are in a resting state, they continue to carry on the same functions as any other living creature. They continue to respire and consume nutrients. It is important to always select fresh, high-quality seed.

When you consider the overall cost of seed in the greater scheme of things, the price is insignificant. It is always best to start with good seed. Once the seed has been purchased, remember care should be taken to keep it in a cool, dry place. Seeds are living things, and exposure to extreme temperatures can greatly reduce their germination. You should remember that bargain seed is usually not a bargain. It has generally been placed on the sale table because it's old and in some cases has been sitting around for many months under less than ideal conditions. There's nothing more frustrating than spending a considerable amount of time and energy preparing a planting bed just to find out the seeds you planted were no good.

If you save your seed from year to year, it is a good idea to store it in a sealed container such as a plastic bag or plastic ware under refrigeration. It is not recommended to freeze your seed unless you know freezing is required to overcome some sort of dormancy. If seed has been stored for several years, it's probably a good idea to take the time to check the germination percentage before the coming gardening season. This can be done very easily by laying out 10 seeds on a sheet of damp paper towel, rolling it up, and placing it in a plastic bag. Place the plastic bag in a warm, not hot, location and check it in about a week. If fewer than 7 seeds out of 10 sprout, you'll probably want to make sure to seed more heavily. If fewer than 4 seeds germinate, it's probably time to dispose of that seed and start off with a fresh batch.

For seed to germinate properly, three environmental conditions must be satisfied. The seed must be provided with an adequate supply of oxygen. Oxygen is important in satisfying the seed's respiratory requirements. Tightly compacted soils or soil saturated with water do not provide the proper environment for good seed germination. Water is the second important part of the germination triangle. Adequate levels of moisture are necessary to activate the chemical processes going on within the seed to initiate the development of the embryo. Finally, soil temperature is critical. All seeds have a temperature range where germination occurs at the maximum rate. Some seed prefer cool soil, while others will only germinate in warm soils. You have to learn enough about the plant you're growing to know what the correct environmental conditions are for proper germination and growth. Some seed may also need light or in some case darkness in order for germination to take place. This, too, will need to be taken into account for those with a light or darkness requirement.

Seed-Grown Vegetables and Herbs

Easily Survive Transplanting
Basil
Broccoli
Brussels sprout
Cabbage
Catnip
Cauliflower
Chamomile
Chard
Chinese cabbage
Chives
Cilantro

Onion
Parsley
Salad burnet
Sorrel
Sweet potato slips
Tomato

Require Care When Transplanting
Borage
Celery
Comfrey
Eggplant

Lettuce

Melon

Pepper

Sweet rocket

Not Usually Transplanted into the Garden

Bean

Calendula

Carrot

Corn, sweet

Cucumber (tend to stop growth)

Dill

Melon

Nasturtium

Okra

Pea

Squash

Direct Seeding

Most vegetables and some herbs and flowers can be planted directly into the garden. There are several ways of planting seed directly into the garden. In all cases, proper soil preparation is critical to your success. A well-prepared seedbed will promote fast germination and healthy growth. The seedbed should be well prepared, loose, and free of any large clods. This is an opportune time to add any necessary soil amendments, fertilizers, and organic matter. Once soil has been well prepared, it should be raked out until smooth and fairly level.

Broadcasting seeding is a common method used for planting vegetables such as mustard, turnip, collards, carrots, and lettuce; herbs like dill, cilantro, and basil; and flowers like larkspur, Johnny-jump-ups, cosmos, or zinnias. Most of these plants require light for germination and as a result need to be planted very close to the surface of the soil. Broadcasted seed should be lightly scattered on the surface of the soil and lightly covered with a loose media such as compost or vermiculite placed on the surface of the soil.

Furrow planting is another common technique used by many gardeners for direct seeding into the garden. It's worth noting at this point that seed should generally be planted at a depth of about 1½ times the diameter of the seed. This means seed like green beans should be planted about ½ to 1

Beans should be seeded 2 inches apart and then thinned to 6 inches apart. Also treat the seed with a bacterial innoculant to promote nitrogen fixation.

VEGETABLE AND HERB SEEDING CHART

Crop	*Planting Time before or after Average Last Spring Frost*	*Planting Time before or after Average First Fall Frost*	*Seeding Depth (Inches)*	*Seed Emergence in Days*	*Optimum Soil Temperature (°F)*	*From Seeding Number of Weeks to Grow Transplants*
Basil	6–15 weeks after (seed or transplants)	NR (not recommended)	¼	3–5	65–85	5–7
Beans	4–12 weeks after (seed)	10–12 weeks before (seed)	1–½	5–10	65–85	NA
Beets	4–6 weeks before (seed)	8–12 weeks before (seed)	½–1	7–10	50–85	NA
Borage	4–15 weeks after (seed or transplants)	NR	¼	7–10	65–85	6–10
Broccoli	2–4 weeks before (transplants)	6–8 weeks before (transplants)	¼–½	3–10	50–85	5–7
Cabbage	2–4 weeks before (transplants)	4–8 weeks before (transplants)	¼–½	4–10	50–85	5–7
Calendula	2–4 weeks before (transplants)	6–8 weeks before (transplants)	¼–½	7–21	55–75	3–5
Carrots	2–4 weeks before up to last frost (seed)	6–10 weeks before (seed)	Lightly covered–¼	12–18	50–85	NA
Cauliflower	NR	6–8 weeks before (transplants)	¼–½	4–10	50–85	5–7
Celery	NR	6–10 weeks before (transplants)	¼–½	9–21	50–65	10–12
Chamomile	4–15 weeks after (transplants)	NR	Lightly covered–¼	7–21	60–85	6–10
Chard, Swiss	2–4 weeks before (seed or transplants)	12–16 weeks before (seed or transplants)	½–¾	7–10	65–85	4–6
Cilantro	2–4 weeks before (seed)	6–8 weeks before (seed)	¼–½	12–18	50–85	6–10
Corn, sweet	1–2 weeks after (some varieties, i.e. Mirai, are cold sensitive and should be planted 4–6 weeks after)	3–4 months before the first frost (pests are more severe with a late crop)	1–2	5–8	65–85	NA
Cucumber	2–4 weeks after (seed)	3–4 months before (seed)	1–2	6–10	65–85	4–6
Dill	2 weeks before to 8 weeks after (for use with pickles) (seed)	4–10 weeks before (best season for dill) (seed)	¼–½	12–18	50–65	NA

Eggplant	4-8 weeks after (transplants)	5 months before (will freeze out easily) (transplants)	1/4	6-10	65-85	6-9
Lettuce	6 weeks before to 2 weeks after (seed or transplants)	12-14 weeks before (from seed), 8-12 weeks before (from transplants)	Lightly covered-¼	6-8	50-65	3-5
Melons	3-6 weeks after (seed)	4-5 months before (seed)	1-2	6-8	65-85	NA
Nasturtium	2 weeks before to 2 weeks after (seed)	8-10 weeks before (seed)	1-2	12-18	50-75	NA
Okra	4-16 weeks after (seed)	NR	1	7-10	65-85	NA
Onion	4-6 weeks before (transplants only)	6-8 weeks before (seed only)	¼	7-10	65-85	4-6
Parsley	4 weeks before to 2 weeks after (transplants only)	8 weeks before (seed or transplants) to 4 weeks after (transplants)	Lightly covered-¼	15-21	50-85	8
Pepper	2-8 weeks after (transplants)	16-20 weeks before (transplants)	¼	9-14	65-85	6-8
Potatoes, sweet	8-12 weeks after (slips)	NR	(slips)	NA	65-85	1-2 for rooting
Radish	6 weeks before the last spring freeze up to average last frost (seed)	8-10 weeks before and sow weekly through the cool season (seed)	¼-½	3-6	50-65	NA
Spinach	NR	8 weeks before until average first frost (seed or transplants)	¼-½	7-12	50-65	NA
Squash	4-6 weeks after last frost	Summer squash varieties: 60-90 days before the first fall frost; winter (storage squash) varieties: 4-5 months before the first fall frost	1-2	4-6	65-85	NA
Tomato	transplants from the last average frost to 8 weeks after	transplants 16-20 weeks before the first fall frost	¼-½	6-12	65-85	5-7
Turnip	6 weeks before to 4 weeks after the last spring frost	plant weekly from 8-12 weeks before the first fall frost and through the cool season	¼	4-8	50-65	NA

* Transplants not recommended.

inch deep, and seed like echinacea should be planted about ⅛ to ¼ inch deep. Furrow planting is done by taking the edge of a hoe, a sharp stick, or other tool to open up a shallow trench in which the seeds are placed. Of course this technique works best on plants that are grown in rows. Once the seed are placed in the furrow, they should be lightly covered with soil, compost, vermiculite, or similar material.

Hill planting is another technique used by kitchen gardeners. Hills are used with vegetables such as melons, pumpkins, and squash or flowers like sweet peas and sunflower. A small hole or depression is made in the planting bed (typically in an area that's been hilled up 8–12 inches high), and three to five seeds are placed in the hole and lightly covered. Once the plants are up and growing, they should be thinned to the appropriate number of plants per hill.

Many gardeners are confused about which plants to grow from seed planted directly in the garden and which to start from transplants. Most garden plants can be transplanted, but those vegetables, herbs, and flowers that germinate easily are good candidates for direct seeding. Root crops such as carrots, turnips, and beets are almost always direct seeded. Transplanting these plants will usually result in damage to the tap root, causing a misshapen or forked root. Herbs and flowers such as dill, larkspur, and sweet peas resent transplanting and perform much better when direct seeded.

Starting Transplants

Should you decide to get into starting your own plants for transplanting, you'll need a few supplies. Almost any type of container will do as long as it will hold enough soil to accommodate the root system of your newly developing plants. Small Styrofoam cups, egg cartons, clay pots, plastic pots, or almost any other similar-type container will work. Be sure that whatever type of container you choose has a drain hole(s) to allow excess water to drain out. To reduce the chance of disease and insects, it's best to start with a good, clean, sterile potting media.

Numerous commercially prepared soil mixes are on the market today. Most of the commercially prepared products are made up of primarily peat and perlite, and for the most part they all will do an adequate job. Many gardeners prefer mixing their own soils, and this will work as well. A good basic potting soil mix might include such ingredients as perlite, vermiculite, Canadian sphagnum peat, fired clay, or coarse sand. You can prepare your own artificial potting medium with little difficulty. The following mixes are suggested for growing a variety of plants:

- Two parts peat, one part perlite, one part coarse sand
- Two parts peat, one part coarse sand
- One part peat, one part coarse sand, one part pine bark
- One part peat, one part pine bark, one part perlite

Cornell Plant Mix

This soilless mix was developed at Cornell University for commercial growers, but it can easily be adapted to home use. This recipe will make approximately a bushel of potting media.

Cornell Foliage Plant Mix
2 bushels sphagnum peat moss
3 bushels vermiculite, No. 2
3 bushels perlite (medium fine)
8 tbsp. ground dolomitic lime
2 tbsp. superphosphate (20% powdered)
3 tbsp. 10-10-10 fertilizer
1 tbsp. iron sulfate
1 tbsp. potassium nitrate

Place the prepared potting media into the selected container and water well. It's important that the soil be thoroughly moistened before planting the seed. Many soil mixtures containing sphagnum peat are difficult to wet initially. Take a little extra time to thoroughly water before planting your seed. Some gardeners like to soak the soil-filled containers in a shallow pan of water in order to completely saturate the soil prior to planting.

Using a dibble (a *dibble* is a planting tool available from some garden supply companies, but a pencil or sharpened chopstick makes an excellent substitute for a "store-bought" dibble), you should open up a small hole in the soil. The hole should be deep enough that the seed is covered with soil mix to a depth of 1 to 1½ times the diameter of the seed. Once the seed or seeds have been placed in the hole, they should be lightly covered with potting soil, or you can use a thin layer of vermiculite. Vermiculite is an excellent material to use since it allows light to penetrate, enhancing the germination of seed like lettuce and many small seed that require light to germinate. In fact, these tiny seed are often planted on the surface, and a light sprinkling of vermiculite is applied mostly to retain moisture.

The newly planted seed should be placed in a well-ventilated area. For those of you fortunate enough to have a greenhouse, this makes an excellent area for starting your own transplants. The rest of us must resort to using areas such as patios, sun porches, a bay window, or even the kitchen counter equipped with fluorescent lights. It's important to realize that high-quality light is needed to produce quality transplants. Most home settings are not bright enough to produce high-quality transplants. For very little money you can install a couple of fluorescent light fixtures equipped with hot white, shop grade, full spectrum, or grow lights to enhance the quality of light and promote healthier, more productive growth.

Once the newly planted seed are up and growing, it's important to provide the seedlings with the proper nutrition. Most commercially available potting mixes, as well as homemade soils, do not provide enough nutrients to promote healthy, vigorous growth. To ensure healthy plants for the garden, it's best to begin applying a water-soluble fertilizer on a weekly basis to the seedlings once they sprout. A wide variety of products are available at your local garden center or nursery. Water-soluble fertilizers are available from a large number of different manufacturers. Most will do a more than adequate job of providing the needed nutrition for your newly developing plants. For those of you interested in using only organic products, you should select one of many liquid organic fertilizers containing kelp, fish emulsion, or seaweed extract.

STARTING YOUR OWN PLANTS FROM CUTTINGS

Many of the plants grown in the kitchen garden can be propagated by taking cuttings. Many gardeners are reluctant to try taking cuttings, but once they experience a little success, they find themselves propagating everything in sight. Cuttings can be used to produce plants to share with friends, to add to your garden, or to save nonhardy plants over the winter for spring planting.

Cuttings involve removing a piece of the mother plant and then treating the piece in such a way as to induce the regeneration of the lost parts of the plant. Many herbs and some fruits and vegetables are propagated by cuttings of stems and roots. New plants can be grown from parts of plants because each living plant cell contains the ability to duplicate all plant parts and functions. There are many types of cuttings, but the stem or tip cutting is the most commonly used for propagating plants found in the kitchen garden.

Stock plant is a common term used to describe the mother plant used in asexual propagation. Stock plants must be in excellent health and should possess characteristics desirable for production of new plants. If you know you are planning to take a number of cuttings from an individual plant, it's a good idea to plan ahead. You can do some things to invigorate your stock plant, so it produces the best cutting material possible. Regular watering, soil fertilization, and even foliar feeding with a dilute fertilizer (most soluble fertilizers list a foliar rate) will perk up your stock plants. Healthy, vigorous shoots make the best cutting material. Several months ahead of collecting cuttings, consider pruning the stock plant severely. Hard pruning results in the production of an abundance of vigorous shoots. Examine the plant for insect and disease problems. Should any problems exist, try to take care of them prior to collecting cutting material.

Most plants commonly grown in the kitchen garden propagate easily from tip or stem cuttings. One of the key ingredients in successful cutting propagation is collecting your propagation material when it is in the proper growth stage. Hardened off new growth is by far the best. Hardened off new growth is the newest flush of growth that has had a chance to fully develop. The stem should still be green, possibly with a few flakes of brown, but not yet in a woody stage of growth. The leaves should be fully developed, and cutting material should be collected after they have advanced beyond a tender succulent stage of growth. Good cutting material can be collected in the southern kitchen garden throughout the spring, summer, and fall as long as the plant continues to produce new vigorous growth.

Cuttings will range in size, depending on the plant, from as small as 2 inches to as large as 6 to 8 inches in length. Each cutting should have at least three to six leaves. Try to make your cut just below a leaf node or bud. Your best root growth will generally appear in the region around the node. When taking cuttings, it's important to protect them from environmental stress. Never allow the cuttings to dry out or wilt—once they have wilted, it is very difficult to revive them. You can protect the cuttings by placing them in a plastic bag or by placing the ends in a bucket of clean water prior to sticking them into the rooting media.

When you get to the potting bench with your cuttings, fill the pots you intend to use with a good rooting media. A wide variety of rooting media can be used. See the section on starting seed for ideas on materials that can be used as a soil media. One of the favorite rooting materials for a wide variety of plants is a 50:50 mix of perlite and vermiculite. This produces a very loose, well-aerated mix that promotes root development on many different herbs and vegetables. Be sure the potting media is watered well prior to sticking any cuttings.

Make a cut just below a leaf node, pull off the leaves on the bottom half of the cutting, and remove any very vigorous, tender new growth. On plants with very large leaves, you may want to cut the leaves in half (measure halfway back from the leaf tip and cut perpendicular to the main leaf vein) to help reduce transpiration. Many plants will benefit from the application of a rooting hormone. There are numerous brands on the market today. Most come in a powdered form using talcum powder as the carrier. Generally the lowest concentration of rooting hormone is more than adequate for the plants we commonly grow in the kitchen garden. If you're not sure whether rooting hormone is necessary to enhance the formation of roots, stick about half the cuttings in without using hormone and the other half with rooting hormone. Pour a small amount of the rooting hormone into a clean container to prevent contamination of the entire bottle of rooting hormone. Dip the base of the stem, including the node area, into the rooting powder. Tap the stem lightly against the side of the container to knock any loose material off prior to sticking.

Poke a hole in the potting media before inserting the cutting to avoid wiping off the rooting hormone. Insert the treated cutting in a moist rooting media and lightly firm the soil in around the cutting.

Cover the container and cutting with a plastic bag tent (support the plastic with wire loops or stakes to keep it from touching the leaves), clear soda bottle, or similar cover to maintain high humidity. Place the mini-greenhouse in a warm, bright (not sunny) location. Check the rooting media every few days to make sure it remains moist. Rooting can take anywhere from a few days up to several months depending on the plant and the time of year. Don't get in a big hurry to examine the cuttings. Repeated removal of the cuttings from the rooting media can greatly inhibit the formation of new roots. After 2 or 3 weeks, test for rooting by gently tugging at the cutting. If there is resistance, rooting has started and the plastic cover can be removed.

Once the cuttings have become well rooted, they can be carefully removed from the rooting media and placed into individual containers. You should begin applying light applications of a water-soluble fertilizer or slow-release fertilizer at this time. Remember most commercial and homemade potting soils are very low in nutrients. Once the plants have become well established, it's time to move them to their new location in the garden.

DIVISION

Division is a method of asexual or vegetative plant propagation. It involves propagating a new plant from a rooted portion of the original plant. As with other methods of vegetative propagation, the propagated plant will have the same characteristics as the parent plant. Division is a simple method of multiplying plants in the kitchen garden. The two basic types of plants propagated by division are those with a clumping growth habit or specialized structures (those plants most gardener consider bulbs).

Division of Specialized Structures

Bulbous plants characteristically have storage organs at or below the soil surface. These specialized organs may be true bulbs, corms, tubers, tuberous roots, rhizomes, or stolons. Bulbs, corms, tubers, rhizomes, and stolons are modified stem tissue, while tuberous roots are made from roots tissue.

Amaryllis, tulips, onions, daffodils, and Easter lilies are examples of plants with true bulbs. Bulbs produce side shoots, bulblets, or offsets from the primary bulb, and the offsets and the primary bulb increase in size with age. Separation of the offsets is an excellent way to propagate bulbous plants.

Gladiolus and crocosmia are examples of corms and are propagated primarily by separation of offsets called cormels from the primary corm. Cormels usually require an additional 1 to 2 years' growth before flowers are produced. Corms are usually harvested after the foliage dies.

Two of the best-known tubers are the Irish potato and caladium. Tubers are modified, underground stems. You can easily propagate tubers by either planting the entire tuber or cutting the tuber into pieces, each containing one or more buds or eyes. Cut surfaces should be allowed to dry overnight before planting to reduce decay.

Rhizomes and stolons are modified, horizontal stems. Rhizomes grow in the soil, while stolons grow horizontally above the soil surface. Most plants that produce rhizomes or stolons are in the grass family (monocots), although some ferns and dicots (most of our nongrass species of plants) produce them. Rhizomes and stolons can be divided to produce additional plants by simply cutting the rhizome or stolon into pieces.

the southern kitchen garden

Clumping Plants

Many plants develop multiple stems or clumps (Shasta daisy, chives, multiplying onion, Mexican mint marigold to mention a few) that can be propagated by division. Herbaceous perennials are most commonly propagated by clump division. This simply involves separating the clump into pieces with adequate roots and shoots for reestablishment. A small clump with one to two shoots and adequate roots for transplanting is all you need to get a new start. Divided pieces should be planted back at the same depth as they were grown originally. Many of these plants—for example, oregano—will root just about everywhere the stems lay on the ground. It's easy to cut these rooted stems off (with roots intact): cut back the foliage to about 6 inches from the start of rooting, and pot them up or move them to another area of the garden.

Plants can be successfully divided almost any time of the year. Division at the wrong time of year is usually successful but may disrupt the natural bloom cycle of the plants in the season to come. In an effort to maintain normal blooming, there is a simple rule of thumb to remember. Plants should be divided in the season opposite their normal blooming season. Early spring–blooming plants should be divided in the fall. Summer- and fall-blooming plants should be divided in the spring. By following this simple rule, you can avoid damaging the plants when they would normally be in bloom.

BUDDING AND GRAFTING

Grafting/budding is a propagation technique where two plants are joined together into one plant. The upper portion of the graft (the scion) becomes the top of the plant; the lower portion (the rootstock) becomes the root system or bottom of the plant. Once you master the technique of grafting, you can create all kinds of unique and unusual combinations of fruits. As long as you start with varieties that are compatible to one another (you must select plants that are very closely related in order for the graft to be successful), you can place a number of different cultivars on the same tree. It's conceivable that you can create combinations that include plums, peaches, and nectarines all on the same tree. Or you may want an apple tree that has several varieties growing on the same trunk. All this is possible using one of the common grafting techniques.

The reason that many fruit trees are grafted is that the varieties we would like to grow for fruit production may not produce a vigorous root system or may have problems with a particular disease or insect. The rootstock is selected because it is very vigorous or tolerates a disease or some other environmental condition common to the area. Sometimes a rootstock is used because it produces a dwarf tree. Many of the tree fruits get very large and as a result don't fit well into the kitchen garden. By grafting a fruit onto a dwarf rootstock, you can create full-size fruit on a much smaller-profile tree. This has definite advantages to the home gardener. Dwarf trees often come into production at a much earlier age, which is another good reason for using dwarf rootstock when planting fruits in the kitchen garden. There are a number of grafting terms that you will want to become familiar with.

Grafting Terms

Budding	A type of grafting that consists of inserting a single bud onto the rootstock
Budding knife	A knife with a short, stiff blade, beveled on one side and with a lifting device on the back of the blade as a separate piece to aid in lifting the bark prior to inserting the bud
Budding tape	A stretchy tape with no adhesive used to wrap the bud after it has been inserted into the bark
Cambium	The growing part of the tree; located between the wood and bark
Cultivar	A particular cultivated plant; sometimes referred to as "variety"
Dormant	The time in the life cycle of the plant when it is not actively growing
Grafting knife	A knife with a short, stiff blade with the bevel on one side to ensure a smooth cut
Rootstock	The part on which the scion is inserted; the part below the graft; the part of a tree that becomes the root system of a grafted or budded tree
Scion	A piece of last year's growth, usually three or four buds; the part inserted into the rootstock
Slipping	When the plant is actively growing and bark separates freely from the wood, cambium will be both on the wood surface and on the inner bark.
Topworking	The operation of cutting back the branches and top of an established tree and budding or grafting part of another tree onto the cut branches

Collecting and Storing Scion Wood

Scions can be selected from last year's growth during the dormant season but before growth begins in the spring. This dormant wood should be wrapped in damp paper towel or newspaper and placed in a sealed plastic bag. It can then be refrigerated for several months prior to the actual grafting. Generally it's a good idea not to store graft wood for more than 4 to 6 months. If you plan on doing late-season grafting (August–November), you may find it better to collect hardened off new growth just prior to grafting.

When to Graft

When you graft will be dependent on the type of plant you plan to graft and the grafting technique that is to be used. It's difficult to recommend the exact months when it's best to perform budding or grafting. For example, citrus can be grafted almost any time during the growing season, using one of three techniques: T-budding, chip budding, or cleft grafting. Fruits like apples, pears, peaches, plums, apricots, and many others can be grafted in the spring or fall using the T-bud or in the winter using a cleft graft.

Tools and Materials Needed

- A good, sharp, stiff-bladed knife
- A fine-tooth saw (for cleft grafting stock 1–4 inches in diameter)
- Pruning shears
- Scion wood (be sure to label the variety). Scion wood can be collected several times of the year. Usually it is gathered in late winter (mid-February is a good time), the ends are dipped in paraffin or a similar sealant, and then the scions are wrapped in damp newspaper and stored in the refrigerator in plastic bags. Scion wood can also be collected during the growing season after mature buds are visible in the leaf axils (usually after the first of June). These scions can be used immediately for budding (it's too late for bark grafts or cleft grafts with these active growth bud sticks), or they can be stored for several weeks in the refrigerator (wrap them in damp newspaper but don't worry about the sealant on these scions, though be sure to place them in plastic bags) and brought out as needed.
- Grafting tape, plant tie tape, or rubber grafting strips
- A cleft-grafting tool and mallet, or a heavy knife (for cleft grafting)
- Small plastic bags and aluminum foil (for bark grafting and cleft grafting)

Note: Budding and grafting knives should be kept very sharp so that as little damage as possible is done to the tissue. Dull knives strip and tear the wood, leaving cuts that do not heal properly.

Methods of Grafting and Budding

- **The Whip and Tongue Graft.** The whip and tongue graft can be used on a wide variety of trees including apples, pears, peaches, nectarines, plums, persimmons, grapes, figs, and many others as long as the branches (or small rootstock) are relatively small (not more than ½ inch in diameter) and the rootstock (or branch) is about the same diameter as the scion of the new cultivar. This is a popular technique with beginners because there is a large amount of cambium surface making contact, and it's held together tightly, giving the propagator greater room for error.

- Holding the rootstock in one hand and holding the knife in the other, pointed away from the body, make a long slanting cut about ¾ to 1½ inches in length. Try to make the slanted cut as smooth and flat as possible. It's important to avoid whittling on the rootstock because this creates a rippled cut rather than the desired flat cut. To create the tongue, place the knife blade about one-third of the way down the long slanting cut and draw the knife toward you, cutting straight into the slanting cut. This second cut should be about ½ to 1 inch long.

Whip and tongue graft.

- Holding the scion wood in one hand and the knife in the other, repeat the previous procedure creating a mirror image of the cuts made on the rootstock.

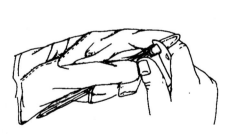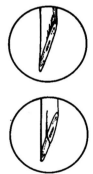

Whip and tongue graft.

- Unless the scion and the rootstock are exactly the same size, be sure the scion is in contact with the cambium layer on just one side. If the ends of either the rootstock or scion extend beyond the heel of the other, don't worry about it—wrapping the entire graft with tape usually provides enough seal to allow the graft to take, regardless, and the overlaps are eventually overgrown. Trying to cut the overlaps off is more likely to shift the cambium out of contact than any "tidying up" advantage it might have.

the southern kitchen garden

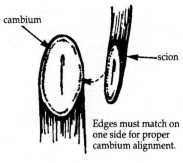

cambium

scion

Edges must match on one side for proper cambium alignment.

Whip and tongue graft.

Whip and tongue graft.

- Using your grafting tape, wrap the two pieces together tightly. It's important for the two cambium layers to be in close contact. Be sure to place enough tension on the plastic tape to ensure good contact, creating a strong graft union. Continue to wrap the tape around the graft union until you have completely covered all cut surfaces. The plastic tape will help to hold the graft together until it heals and retains moisture without keeping the graft too wet. Note: Current research has shown that grafting tape or plant tie tape is much better than using the older method of string and grafting wax. The grafting wax tends to work its way into cracks and crevices, inhibiting the formation of a strong graft union.
- In 4 to 6 six weeks the graft should have healed well. Once new growth is noted and the graft union has had an opportunity to heal, the tape can be removed. You may want to place a stake next to or tied onto the stock below the graft with these newly developing grafts for the first season to help provide additional support and prevent the graft from being broken by roosting birds or strong winds. Use tape and a piece of foam packing between the developing scion and the stake to secure the graft.
- The whip and tongue graft is best attempted when both the rootstock and the scion are dormant.

- **The Cleft Graft.** The cleft graft is one of the simplest and most popular forms of grafting. It is commonly used for topworking established flowering and fruiting trees (apples, cherries, pears, and peaches) in order to change or add varieties. Cleft grafting can also be used to graft small evergreen plants such as camellias and citrus. This type of grafting is usually done during the winter and early spring while both scion and rootstock are still dormant, but it can be a very successful technique for grafting citrus throughout the year. Cleft grafting may be performed on the main trunk or on side branches.

    When cleft grafting established trees, the rootstock will usually be somewhere between 4 and 6 inches in diameter. When cleft grafting citrus or camellias the rootstock is worked when it is much smaller—usually ¼ to ½ inch in diameter. The scion should be about ¼ to ⅜ inch in diameter, straight, and long enough to have at least three buds.

- The rootstock should be cut off with a clean, smooth cut perpendicular to the trunk or branch. Place the cleft grafting tool or heavy knife in the center of the cut-off portion and make a downward split in the rootstock about 1½ to 3 inches deep. Remove the cleft grafting tool. When grafting larger trees, you may find it necessary to drive a screwdriver or wedge into the split to hold it open enough to allow insertion of the scion.
- Holding the scion in one hand and the knife in the other, make a long slanted cut on one side of the scion wood. This slanted cut should be approximately 1 to 2 inches in length. It may take several tries before you get a long, smooth, clean, flat cut. It's important that the cut be flat, so try to avoid whittling. Turn the scion wood over and make another long slanted cut creating a wedge—wider on the outside edge of the scion to make it fit better in the cleft near the outer edge where the rootstock cambium is located.
- Insert the scion into the rootstock split or cleft, lining up the outside edge of the scion with the cambium layer of the rootstock. It's important to remember that when grafting larger trees, the rootstock bark may be very thick. This means the scion will need to be moved in the thickness of the rootstock bark in order for the cambium layer of the scion and the rootstock to line up.
- If a screwdriver or wedge was used to hold open the split, remove it at this time. The pressure of the rootstock pushing in should hold the scion in place. When using the cleft grafting technique on smaller trees (under 1 inch in diameter), you should use your grafting tape to wrap the cut surfaces completely. Apply tension to the tape to help pull the sides of the rootstock in firmly against the scion. Once the graft is wrapped completely with the tape, covering all cut surfaces, tie it off with a half hitch. When using the cleft grafting technique on larger trees, you will need to cover the split with a small piece of aluminum foil (the aluminum foil helps to reflect light, reducing heat buildup around the graft) followed by a small plastic bag. One corner of the bag can be cut with your knife to allow the scion to stick out of the bag. Use a small length of plant tie tape or grafting tape to tie around the top the bag where the scion sticks out and at the bottom of the bag to seal moisture in around the graft union.
- Scions that are growing vigorously will need attention to prevent breakage by birds, and wind. Either tie the scion to a supporting stake, or pinch back the tips before growth becomes excessively long to reduce air resistance.
- When grafting very large branches or trunks you may find it desirable to insert two scions, one on each side of the split trunk. If both scions are successful you will need to remove one of them after they are well established to prevent overcrowding and the development of a narrow crotch. Be sure to remove any suckers that develop below the graft. These

suckers may overgrow the scion resulting in weak growth or possible loss of the graft. Continue selecting and training the graft for the next several years until you have developed the framework and growth habit desired.

- **T-Budding.** T-Budding differs from other forms of grafting in that only a single bud is used as the scion rather than a section of stem. It is the most commonly used method for fruit tree production in the nursery, but it can also be used for reworking the limbs of many plants including plum, cherry, apricot, and peach as well as young apple and pear trees.

  T-budding is used whenever the bark of the rootstock slips easily (generally late spring and fall during an active growth period). This means that the cambium is actively growing, and the bark can be peeled easily from the wood with little effort or damage. The first step involves cutting the bud sticks of the desired cultivar from strong shoots of the present season's growth. The buds located in the leaf axils should be mature, plump, and well formed. They can be collected during the dormant season and stored for future use or from mature new growth at the time of budding.

T-budding.

- After determining that the rootstock is actively growing and the bark is slipping, make a ¾- to 1½-inch vertical cut on the rootstock making sure you cut completely through the bark to the cambium.
- Make a perpendicular cut at the upper end of the vertical cut forming a T. In areas with heavy rainfall during the grafting season, or in species in which the rootstock is likely to "bleed" heavily, an upside-down or inverted T-bud can be used to prevent water or sap from pooling in the graft. In this case, the horizontal cut is made at the bottom of the vertical cut.
- With the edge of the knife carefully pry the bark from the wood, creating a pocket into which the bud shield can be placed. Care should be taken not to tear the flaps of bark in the process of opening up the pocket.
- Hold the bud stick in one hand; place the knife blade below the bud, cut a bud from bud stick with a thin piece of attached wood. The cut should begin about ¼ to ½ inch below the bud and should go deep enough into the wood so that when the cut is finished about ½ inch above the bud, the bark and a small sliver of wood are cut off. A perpendicular cut across the

top of the upward cut will separate the bud from the bud stick. The result is called a *bud shield*. If the bud stick was collected during the growing season, a ¼-inch piece of leaf petiole is left attached to serve as a handle since it is best not to touch the cut surfaces with your fingers.

- Slide the bud shield into the opened pocket on the rootstock. As long as the bark is slipping, you'll find it very easy to slip the bud into the T-shaped cut. If the bud shield should extend above the top of the T, just trim off the excess bark.

- Starting from below the bud, begin wrapping the T-shaped cut and the bud with a piece of grafting tape, plant tie tape, or grafting rubber. Try to completely cover all cut areas. Avoid covering the actual bud with the tape unless you are certain to remove it after several weeks of healing.

- Late spring buds should be allowed to heal for about 6 weeks. After the bud is well healed, make a slanted cut to remove the top portion of the rootstock just above the bud, which will force the bud to begin growing. The tape can be removed at this time. For fall buds you should wait until spring to force growth by cutting the rootstock just above the T-bud. Immediately after inserting the bud in the fall, however, you may want to break over the tips of the budded branches to reduce apical dominance and help set the bud.

- Aftercare includes staking the newly developing shoot (the forced T-bud) and pinching off the suckers that sprout on the rootstock. Once the bud has made sufficient growth, the development of suckers will decrease and eventually stop.

■ **Bark Graft.** Bark grafting is commonly used to topwork flowering and fruiting trees. In contrast to cleft grafting, which is done primarily during the dormant season, this technique should be attempted in the spring or early summer when the bark slips easily from the wood.

- The rootstock should be cut off, using a sharp saw, at a point where the graft is to be placed. This is usually where the trunk or limb is 1 to 2 inches in diameter. Try to make as clean a cut as possible.

- Use a sharp knife to remove and clean up any frayed or torn bark and cambium tissue.

- Starting at the cut-off surface of the rootstock, make a vertical cut through the bark where the scion will be inserted. The vertical cut should be about 2 inches long. On rootstock larger than 3 inches in diameter, you may want to place more than one scion on the stock.

- Cut the base of each scion to a 1½- to 2-inch tapered wedge on one side only.

- Loosen the bark slightly on both sides of the vertical cut on the rootstock with the point of the knife and insert the scion so that the wedge-shaped tapered surface of the scion is against the exposed wood of the rootstock. Push the scion firmly down into place beneath the two flaps of bark. Hold the scion in place by driving one or two wire nails through scion and into the wood of the rootstock. On large rootstocks, it is possible to space several bark grafts around the circumference.

- Seal all cut surfaces with grafting tape, followed by a layer of aluminum foil.
- Once the scion has begun to grow you will want to place a stake on the rootstock and tie the new shoots to it for added support.

■ **Inlay Bark Graft.** Inlay grafting is one of the best and most popular systems of propagating pecans. It has also been successfully used on walnuts, apples, pears, grapes, rabbiteye blueberries, and persimmons. This technique uses an inlay cut formed by two parallel cuts made through the bark on the rootstock to provide a slot or inlay that perfectly fits the cut scion.

- Using the rootstock trunk or side limbs, make a smooth cut at 2 to 4 inches in diameter. Leave one or two side branches below the cut to serve as survival limbs and to keep the trunk from sunburning. Cut straight across the trunk or limb with a sharp saw just as recommended for the traditional bark graft. If the cut is uneven or tears down a strip of bark, recut the trunk/limb below the tear.
- If the old bark is rough, shave it down to smooth bark, forming a clean shield. Leave the bark as thick as possible to securely hold the graft. Do not cut through the bark into the wood.
- Using a sharp knife, and firmly holding the knife in a closed fist, cut the graft stick downward and then out to the end of the scion with numerous thin slices until you have made a long, flat cut that is parallel to the back of the scion. The long cut can be from 1½ to 3 inches long and necessitates a shoulder before the long, smooth cut begins. The scion will push down into the inlay and rest on this shoulder.
- Turn the stick around and make a back cut that is ½-inch long, at about a 45° angle to create a wedge. This makes it easier to insert the graft stick into the inlay and provides additional cambium contact.
- Place the long cut surface of the graft stick against the clean shield of smooth bark on the rootstock. Hold the scion firmly in place with the left thumb. Begin the first inlay cut at the top of the stock on the right side of the graft stick. Cut through the bark down into the wood (it will only cut slightly past the cambium tissue and then the hardwood prevents cutting any deeper). Draw the knife straight down the right side of the graft stick to within ¾ inch of the bottom of the graft stick. It is very important to make this cut straight into the bark. Do not angle the knife to the left or right, or the inlay will be too narrow or too wide.

- Hold the scion in position with the thumb of the right hand. Do not allow the graft to move after the right side inlay cut has been made. Bring the left hand around the back of the rootstock, and anchor the scion with the first three fingers of the left hand and hold in the same exact position. Make the second inlay cut on the left side of the scion, cutting straight into the bark just as you did on the right side.
- The two parallel inlay cuts through the bark should be exactly the same width and shape as the scion. If you slanted your blade in making the cut, the channel may be too narrow. Some propagators like to stop the cut ¼ to ½ inch before the end of the scion. Apparently if the scion is pushed into this area and some tearing results, there is more rapid healing.
- Peel the bark flap ½ inch down between the two parallel inlay cuts. Slide the scion between the bark and wood of the rootstock. There should be no air space between the scion and the two inlay cuts. If the bark does not easily separate from the wood, the cambium is not slipping, and you will need to wait until the tree is in active growth. Apply firm but gentle pressure on top of the graft until it is forced into the inlay slot.
- Once the graft stick is inserted, press the bark flap against the graft stick with the thumb of the right hand to firmly hold the graft stick in the slot.
- The graft can be secured by any one of several methods: 18-gauge ¾-inch nails, ⅝-inch flat point staples in a vertical position, or grafting tape can all be used successfully.
- Wrap the stump with aluminum foil to help reflect the sun and reduce the buildup of heat around the graft. The bottom of the foil fits right under the lowest bud.

Inlay bark graft. Cuts are made on either side of the scion and the scion is slipped into the channel made by these cuts and secured with 18-gauge nails or ⅝- or ⁵⁄₁₆-inch flat point staples.

- Cut off one corner of a pint- or quart-sized polyethylene bag. Slip the bag over the scion, and gently pull it down until the cut corner rests below the lowest bud and above the slant cut.
- Tie the polyethylene bag at the cut corner around the graft stick just below the lowest bud and above the slant cut to keep the scion from drying out. Tie the bottom of the bag with grafting tape to further seal moisture in and air out.

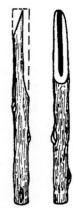

Inlay bark graft chisel cut on the scion.

The buds on the scion should begin to grow in about 6 weeks. Remove the polyethylene bag and foil when the shoots are over 6 inches long. Keep these shoots pruned back to only 24 inches to prevent wind blowouts. After a year, select the strongest shoot on the graft stick and remove all others. After 2 or 3 years, when three-fourths or the entire trunk is covered with overgrowth, remove all shoots below the graft.

appendix: garden plans

Except for your first garden after the initial construction phase, you rarely have a clean slate of garden beds to design a planting plan for. Instead, you are constantly transitioning from crop to crop. Mid- to late summer is one of the most difficult times to keep the garden producing, so you may choose to clean out and clean up at this time in preparation for the fall garden. The very nature of the kitchen garden, however, is intensive, so it is not impossible for gardeners in the South to have crops either just planted or maturing 12 months of the year. Even during the dreaded months of July–September, crops like southern peas, cucumbers, yard-long beans, climbing spinach, tomatillos, eggplant, and hot peppers can thrive with plenty of water and nutrients. Add a few hot weather flowers like gomphrena and zinnia to "ice the cake," and while you may have to avoid working in the garden during midday, it can be a joy in the morning and evening.

SPRING GARDEN

March and April are the big planting months for these warm season vegetables. The most productive and popular vegetables are bush beans, squash, tomatoes, and peppers, but you may want to find room for eggplants, pole beans, or cucumbers (if you have a trellis in one of the beds). These spring-planted crops can often be replanted later in the season (June–September, depending on the crop) for a fall harvest. For example, tomatoes may need to be set out in late June/early July to mature in time for fall while bush beans are great planted from late August through the first week of September to produce in the cooler weather of fall. Spring-planted pepper and eggplants often survive the summer to produce again in the fall.

Looking at our sample plan for a spring garden, bed 1 is planted to tomatoes, possibly with an eggplant or pepper plant included. By late July, the tomatoes may have run their course and your family is tired of eggplant. You could replant with a hot weather crop like southern peas or you could let the bed lay fallow for a fall-planted crop like Chinese cabbage, radishes, and onions. If you decide to

Spring Kitchen Garden

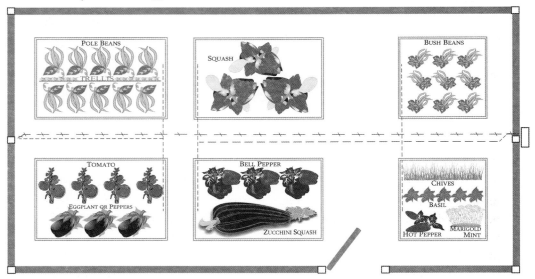

replant, you always run the risk that the summer crop won't mature in time to allow a proper planting schedule for the cool season crops.

Garden bed 2 with bell peppers and zucchini squash will need to be at least partially reworked by mid- to late summer. The peppers can usually be coaxed into fall production, but the zucchini will be growing in the aisles by this time and it will likely be home to a nice crop of vine borers, too. Chances are you're sick of zucchini, the freezer is half full of the stuff, and the neighbors run when they see you head out with plastic bags bulging with squash. Leave the zucchini portion fallow for cauliflower transplants in September/October, and expect to remove the peppers in time to plant kale, collards, and other winter-tough cole (*cole* is a term synonymous with *cabbage family*) crops later in the fall.

Bed 3, the herb bed, will still have chives through the summer (though they really thrive in the fall/winter), basil will be a main crop, and there should be room for a hot pepper plant (one jalapeño or serrano is usually more than enough) and a perennial plant of Mexican marigold mint (*Tagetes lucida*) or rosemary. In the fall, the basil and pepper can give way to cilantro, parsley, thyme, savory, and dill.

Garden bed 4 includes a trellis to take advantage of vertical gardening space. In the spring garden, pole beans are a good choice. When heat and spider mites begin to take a toll on the beans, replant with cucumbers (some may want to plant the trellis half with cucumbers at the same time pole beans are planted) or yard-long beans, climbing spinach, or "pantyhose" melons (muskmelons tied up in a piece of pantyhose).

Garden bed 5 is planted to a vigorous hybrid squash like Dixie crookneck. You will likely be suffering from squash overload by late summer, so clean this bed out, renew with fresh organic matter (preferably compost), and plan to dedicate this bed to broccoli or a similar cool season crop in the fall.

Bed 6 will be solid with bush beans through early summer. As production declines, pull out the plants, add more organic matter, and plant southern peas. Stick with the bush varieties so you can be finished harvesting in time to plant a fall salad garden in this bed.

FALL GARDEN

The transition to fall crops begins in September/October, and this can be a time of drought and brutal heat. It can also be a time of early cold fronts and constant rain but, mostly we prepare for the heat and dry weather. One of the most useful accessories to come along in years is fiber row cover. This spun polypropylene fabric may have begun its career as a liner for diapers, but it has also proven to be a savior in the garden. We place it over the rows of new transplants like broccoli or lettuce, and it protects them from the drying effect of the wind and shades out about 10% of the sun. Some gardeners install hoops of plastic pipe; others just allow this lightweight fabric to float over the plants. Anchor it along the edges with boards, bricks, or blocks, and you have an intensive care nursery to get these tender plants off to a good start in the heat. In the spring, we use this same material to wrap around tomato cages for wind protection. It can also help to exclude virus-carrying insects from getting to the young plants.

Just because these crops grow during cool weather, don't think they won't need much fertilizer. Most fall crops are heavy feeders and will need frequent applications of fertilizer to produce a top-quality product.

Kitchen garden bed 1 we're reserving for Asian vegetable like Chinese cabbage and bok choy. There should also be room for a row of short-day bulbing onions like Burgundy or Texas SuperSweet (or plant multiplying onions to go with the stir-fry veggies). In between plant radishes and/or carrots.

Bed 2 is our cauliflower bed, but it can also be planted with kale, collards, brussels sprouts, or cabbage. If you insist that your garden be pretty as well as tasty, then be sure to include the new kale—Redbor. This variety develops into 3 feet of burgundy frills.

The herb bed (bed 3) can be quickly transformed into cool season crops with a trip to the local nursery. Basil, which will have dominated the summer herb bed, will start to look rather sick when temperatures begin to drop into the 40s at night. Pull out the basil and set transplants of thyme, savory, and oregano into the bed replenished with a fresh layer of compost. Dill and cilantro can be set out as transplants, or they grow easily from seed. Within weeks you're ready to show off the new cool season herb bed.

Fall Kitchen Garden

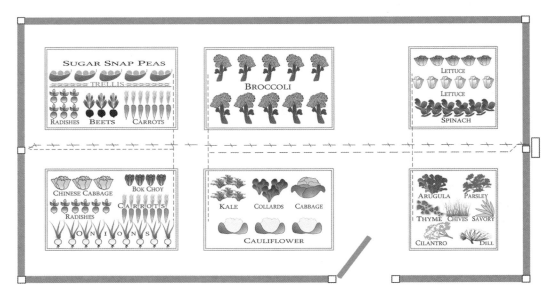

Kitchen garden bed 4 (with trellis) features sugar snap edible-podded peas for most of the winter/spring period. Some years a hard freeze may take them out but they can be replanted in February. The rest of the bed is great for carrots, beets, turnips, mustard, and radishes.

Bed 5 is our broccoli bed, and six to eight plants will likely dominate this planting area. Be sure to plant varieties like Gypsy, Packman, or Southern Comet that produce lots of side sprouts to ensure a winter-long harvest.

Finally, bed 6 is the salad bed. Two rows of lettuce—perhaps one with romaine and another with leaf lettuce—plus a row of spinach should keep you in salads until the plants bolt to seed in the spring.

These garden plans are just suggestions. Feel free to move them around or modify the planting rows. Maybe you want half a row of spinach and half of corn salad (mache). So many garden plants and so little space and time!

To be honest, we've added to our kitchen garden twice. The first time it was 8 × 32 feet (one railroad tie wide by four long) so we could plant more tomatoes and some okra. The second time we wanted to grow sweet corn. A small patch the year prior had us salivating for more. This time we went two wide by four long. The sweet corn was followed by a crop of pumpkins and winter squash (all space gobbling crops in a small kitchen garden). You have to be careful, or your kitchen garden can become a truck garden.

Though we haven't included flowers in our suggested crop rotations, they are almost always present in our garden. Zinnias thrive in hot weather and will literally pull butterflies out of the sky. Some of those fallow areas could be planted to zinnias. The hard part is taking them out when you need to plant broccoli and other veggies. Gomphrena and tithonia are also summer-tough flowers. In the winter violas and nasturtiums are both pretty and edible.

Our orchard is separate from the kitchen garden but close to the house. It includes apples, pears, figs, pomegranates, jujubes, peaches, nectarines, plums, and persimmons. Many trees have been grafted to multiple varieties—something of a management nightmare, but we like to experiment. Trees are heavily mulched with compost in the spring and with grass clippings through the summer. A drip irrigation system keeps them watered, and with the exception of stone fruits (peaches, nectarines, and plums), we use low-toxicity pesticides like neem oil to discourage the grasshoppers. Stone fruits, with their susceptibility to brown rot fungus and plum curculio, require that we spray more diligently so that we don't have to eat around the worms or lose the crop to the brown mush that is brown rot.

GARDENING INTERNET SITES

This is just a sprinkling of what is available today on the Internet in the gardening realm. Hopefully these will be enough to whet your appetite for virtual gardening. There are URLs for general gardening information, master gardeners around the country, places to visit, and horticultural organizations (this is a good place to start if you need information on a specific plant because these societies maintain good link lists to other sites). There are also some URLs if you are looking for good information on youth gardening. If you don't find what you are looking for, try using a general search engine, or call your county extension agent, who will be happy to assist you in finding what you are looking for.

General Gardening Information

Alabama Extension—Home & Garden
www.aces.edu/makemenu.php3?mlevel=11

Clemson (South Carolina) Extension
www.clemson.edu/extension/

Gardening in the Gulf South
members.aol.com/cucryer/lagardeners.html

Horticulture in Virtual Perspective
hcs.osu.edu

iVillage Garden Web
gardenweb.com

Le Jardin Ombragé (ginger information)
www.gingersrus.com

LSU Ag Center
www.agctr.lsu.edu/

Mississippi Extension
msucares.com/

Museum of Garden History
www.compulink.co.uk/~museumgh

North Carolina Extension
www.ces.ncsu.edu

Oklahoma State University Entomology and
    Plant Pathology
www.ento.okstate.edu

Organization of Rare Fruit Growers
userwww.sfsu.edu

Seed Catalog Source
www.b-and-t-world-seeds.com

Southern Gardening
www.southerngardening.com

Texas A&M Aggie Horticulture
aggie-horticulture.tamu.edu

Texas A&M Entomology
entowww.tamu.edu

Texas Plant Disease Handbook
plantpathology.tamu.edu/Texlab/index.htm

University of Arkansas Extension
www.uaex.edu/

University of Florida Extension
edis.ifas.ufl.edu

University of Georgia Extension
www.caes.uga.edu/extension

Master Gardeners

Harris County Master Gardener Association
harris-cnty.tamu.edu/mg

Master Gardener Programs in the USA
www.hal-pc.org/~trobb/mastgar.html

Texas Master Gardeners
aggie-horticulture.tamu.edu/mastergd/
   mg.html

Places to Visit

Atlanta Botanical Garden (Georgia)
www.atlantabotanicalgarden.org

Birmingham Botanical Gardens (Alabama)
www.bbgardens.org

Brooklyn Botanic Garden (New York)
www.bbg.org

Callaway Gardens (Georgia)
www.callawaygardens.com

Dallas Arboretum (Texas)
www.dallasarboretum.org

Daniel Stowe Botanical Garden (North
   Carolina)
www.stowegarden.org

JC Raulston Arboretum (North Carolina)
arb.ncsu.edu

Longwood Gardens (Delaware)
www.longwoodgardens.org

Marie Selby Botanical Garden (Florida)
www.selby.org

Mercer Arboretum and Botanic Gardens
   (Texas)
www.hcp4.net/mercer/general.htm

Moody Gardens (Texas)
www.moodygardens.com

The National Garden (Washington, D.C.)
www.nationalgarden.org

San Antonio Botanical Gardens (Texas)
www.sabot.org

State Botanical Garden of Georgia
www.uga.edu/~botgarden

Stephen F. Austin University Mast
   Arboretum (Texas)
arboretum.sfasu.edu

U.S. Botanic Garden (Washington, D.C.)
www.usbg.gov

Zilker Botanical Garden (Texas)
www.zilker-garden.org

Horticultural Organizations

American Horticultural Society
www.ahs.org

American Society for Horticultural Science
www.ashs.org

The Herb Society—United Kingdom
www.henriettesherbal.com

National Gardening Association
www.garden.org

The Mushroom Council
www.mushroomcouncil.com

Youth Gardening

Composting for Kids
Aggie-horticulture.tamu.edu/sustainable/
 slidesets/kidscompost/cover.html

Nutrition in the Garden
aggie-horticulture.tamu.edu/nutrition/
 index/index.html

Junior Master Gardener Program
Juniormastergardener.tamu.edu

Youth Gardening Information Source
ag.arizona.edu/maricopa/garden/html/
 youth/youth.htm

KinderGarden
aggie-horticulture.tamu.edu/kindergarden/
 kinder.htm

MAIL-ORDER RESOURCES

This is a partial list of firms selling plants and gardening supplies. The inclusion of a firm does not guarantee reliability, and an absence does not imply disapproval. This information was viable at the time this book was written; the authors are not responsible for changes of address and so forth or for discontinued firms or varieties.

A. M. Leonard, Inc.
241 Fox Drive, PO Box 816, Piqua, OH
 45356
Phone: 800-543-8955
Fax: 800-433-0633
Website: www.amleo.com
Ever wonder where to buy a grafting knife, a
 dibble, or some other special garden
 tool? This is the place.

Bob Wells Nursery
17160 CR 4100, Lindale, TX 75771
Phone: 903-882-3550
Fax: 903-882-8030
E-mail: bobwellsnursery@gmail.com
Website: www.bobwellsnursery.com
Offers nut, fruit, and shade trees, plus berries,
 grapes, roses, and flowering shrubs.

Edible Landscaping
PO Box 77, Afton, VA 22920
Phone: 800-524-4156
Fax: 434-361-1916
E-mail: info@ediblelandscaping.com
Website: www.eat-it.com

Source for unusual fruits, nice assortment of
 figs, even offers a few mayhaws.

Flowerfield Enterprises
10332 Shaver Road, Kalamazoo, MI 49024
Phone: 616-327-0108
Fax: 616-327-7009
Website: www.wormwoman.com
Source for earthworms and vermiculture
 supplies.

The Foodcrafter's Supply Catalog
PO Box 442, Waukon, IA 52172-0442
Phone: 800-776-0575
Website: www.kitchenkraft.com
Offers hard-to-find kitchen tools, canning
 supplies, herbal preservation supplies.

Ison Nursery and Vineyard
PO Box 190, Brooks, GA 30205
Ph orders: 800-733-0324
Phone: 770-599-6970
Website: www.isons.com
Looking for muscadine grapes? This is the
 place.

Louisiana Nursery
5853 Hwy. 182, Opelousas, LA 70570
Phone: 337-948-3696
Fax: 337-942-6404
Fascinating source for rare landscape plants; several catalogs are available. Main catalog: $7.00. Lots of rare plants, including the goumi.

Raintree Nursery
391 Butts Road, Morton, WA 98356-9700
Phone: 360-496-6400
Fax: 888-770-8358
E-mail: order@raintreenursery.com
Website: raintreenursery.com
Source for lots of rare fruit varieties, including Petite Negri fig.

Rincon-Vitova Insectaries, Inc.
PO Box 1555, Ventura, CA 93002-1555
Website: www.rinconvitova.com
Catalog of beneficial insects, predators and parasitoids, monitoring tools, and more.

Roger and Shirley Meyer Nursery
16531 Mt. Shelley, Fountain Valley, CA 92708
Phone: 714-839-0796
E-mail: exoticfruit@95net.com
This is your source for jujubes and lots of other rare fruits.

Sandy Mush Herbs
316 Surrett Cove Rd., Leicester, NC 28748-5517
Phone: 828-683-2014
E-mail: info@sandymushherbs.com
Website: www.sandymushherbs.com
Mail-order herbs including 94 varieties of scented geraniums.

Womack Nursery Co.
2551 Hwy 6, De Leon, TX 76444-9631
Phone: 254-893-6497
Fax 254-893-3400
Website: www.womacknursery.com
Source for pecan and fruit trees, pecan graftwood, plus landscape trees, shrubs, and roses.

SEED CATALOGS

This is a partial list of firms selling seeds, plants, sprouting supplies, and mushroom kits. The inclusion of a firm does not guarantee reliability, and an absence does not imply disapproval. These addresses were viable at the time this book was written; the authors are not responsible for changes of address or discontinued firms or varieties.

Baker Creek Heirloom Seeds
2278 Baker Creek Road, Mansfield, MO 65704
Phone: 417-924-8917
Website: www.rareseeds.com
Lots of old but new rare seeds—interesting reading.

Bountiful Gardens
18001 Shafer Ranch Road, Willits, CA 95490-9626
Phone: 707-459-6410
Fax: 707-459-1925
E-mail: bountiful@sonic.net
Website: www.bountifulgardens.org

Source for open-pollinated and untreated seeds.

Burpee (W. Atlee) & Co.
300 Park Ave., Warminster, PA 18991-0001
Phone: 800-888-1447
Fax 800-487-5530
Website: www.burpee.com
Free catalog. Lots of exclusive and proprietary varieties. Many more specialty vegetables—like Charantai melons, Purple Blush eggplant, and Roly Poly squash—are offered than used to be available from this quality seed company. Useful when planning your garden.

The Chile Pepper Institute
NMSU, Box 30003, Dept. 3Q, Las Cruces,
    NM 88003
Phone: 505-646-3028
E-mail: hotchile@nmsu.edu
Website: www.chilepepperinstitute.org/
A source for hot pepper seeds and
    information.

The Cook's Garden
PO Box C5030, Warminster, PA 18974
Phone: 800-457-9703
Website: www.cooksgarden.com
Free catalog. Great source for gourmet
    varieties. Variety descriptions are
    appetite inspiring, and so are the
    recipes.

Evergreen Y. H. Enterprises
PO Box 17538, Anaheim, CA 92817
Phone: 714-637-5769
Fax 714-637-5769
E-mail: EEseeds@aol.com
Website: evergreenseeds.com
Source for Asian vegetable seeds, books, and
    cooking supplies.

Field & Forest Products
N3296 Kozuzek Road, Peshtigo, WI 54157
Phone: 800-792-6220 or 715-582-4997
Fax: 715-582-0181
Website: www.fieldforest.net
Source for mushroom spawn and growing
    supplies.

Fungi Perfecti LLC
PO Box 7634, Olympia, WA 98507
Phone: 800-780-9126 (orders), 360-426-
    9292
Fax: 360-426-9377
E-mail: info@fungi.com
Website: www.fungi.com
From mushroom kits to books and
    medicinals—they have it all.

Gardener's Supply Co.
128 Intervale Road, Burlington, VT 05401
Phone: 800-863-1700
Fax: 800-551-6712
E-mail: info@gardeners.com

Website: www.gardeners.com
Great source for supplies including organic
    pest controls.

Gourmet and Mushroom Products
PO Box 515, Grafton, CA 95444
Phone: 707-829-7301
Website: www.gmushrooms.com
Mushroom kits, books, and more.

Harris Seeds
355 Paul Rd., PO Box 24966, Rochester,
    NY 14692-0966
Phone: 800-514-4441
Fax: 716-442-9386
Website: www.harrisseeds.com
Free catalog. Good historical and growing
    tips for most vegetables. Also features
    "Customer Favorite" varieties, and
    many commercial and even specialty
    selections like the Mexican herb
    epazote.

Hudson (J. L.), Seedsman
Star Route 2, Box 337, La Honda, CA
    94020
Website and online catalog:
    www.jlhudsonseeds.net/catalog.htm
Exhaustive catalog of many plant seeds from
    shrubs to vegetables.

Irish Eyes, Garden City Seed
5045 Robinson Canyon Road, Ellenburg,
    WA 98926
This company specializes in a large selection
    of potatoes including unusual varieties
    and heirlooms. Their catalog includes a
    good selection of vegetable seed, flowers,
    herbs, fertilizers, beneficial insects,
    garden supplies, tools, mushrooms kits,
    and more.

Johnny's Selected Seeds
955 Benton Avenue, Winslow, ME 04901-
    2601
Phone: 877-564-6697
Fax: 800-738-6314
Website: www.johnnyseeds.com
Free catalog. Many heirloom and open-
    pollinated varieties as well as hybrids.

This is a fun catalog with good prices and service.

John Scheepers Kitchen Garden Seeds
23 Tulip Drive, PO Box 638, Bantam, CT 06750-0638
Phone: 860-567-6086
Fax: 860-567-5323
Website: www.kitchengardenseeds.com
Seeds from around the world especially for kitchen gardens.

Kitazawa Seed Co.
PO Box 13220, Oakland, CA 94661-3220
Phone: 510-595-1188
Fax: 510-595-1860
E-mail: kitaseed@pacbell.net
Website: www.kitazawaseed.com
Asian seeds, books, and cooking supplies.

Mushroom Adventures
355 Serrano Drive, Suite 9-J, San Francisco, CA 94132
Phone: 415-586-4082
Website: www.mushroomadventures.com
Mushroom kits and more.

Mushroom People
560 Farm Road, PO Box 220, Summertown, TN 38483-0220
E-mail: mushroom@the farm.org
Website: www.mushroompeople.com

New Dimension Seed
PO Box 1294, Scappoose, OR 97056
Phone: 503-577-9382
Fax: 503-543-4690
Website: www.newdimensionseed.com
More Asian seeds.

Nichols Garden Nursery
1190 North Pacific Hwy., Albany, OR 97321
Phone: 541-928-9280; orders, 800-422-3985
E-mail: Nichols@gardennursery.com
Website: www.nicholsgardennursery.com
Great source for herbs, Asian, European vegetables, and broccoli seeds for sprouting.

Park Seed Co.
1 Parkton Ave., Greenwood, SC 29647-0001
Phone: 800-845-3369
Fax: 864-941-4206
E-mail: info@parkseed.com
Website: www.parkseed.com
Free catalog. Good service and quality.

Peaceful Valley Farm Supply
PO Box 2209, Grass Valley, CA 95945
Phone: 530-272-4769; orders, 888-784-1722
Fax: 530-272-4794
Catalog: $2.00. Source for organic gardening supplies and organically grown, open-pollinated seeds.

Pepper Joe's, Inc.
1650 Pembrooke Road, Norristown, PA 19403
Website: www.pepperjoe.com
Catalog: $2.00. Source of unusual peppers and tomatoes.

Pinetree Garden Seeds
Box 300, New Gloucester, ME 04260
Phone: 207-926-3400
E-mail: pinetree@superseeds.com
Website: www.superseeds.com
Free catalog. Small, less expensive seed packets; extensive selection of books, too.

Plants of the Southwest
1812 Second St., Santa Fe, NM 87501
Phone: 800-788-7333
Fax 505-438-8800
E-mail: mark@plantsofthesouthwest.com
Website: www.plantsofthesouthwest.com
Catalog: $1.00. Another source for chiles and southwestern plants, including grasses.

Redwood City Seed Co.
PO Box 361, Redwood City, CA 94064
Phone: 650-325-7333
Website: www.ecoseeds.com
Free catalog. Source for unusual vegetables, including Asian and Mexican special collections.

Renee's Garden
7389 West Zayante Rd., Felton, CA 95018
Phone: 888-880-7228
Fax: 831-335-7227
Website: Reneesgarden.com
Source for gourmet vegetable varieties.

Richters Herbs
357 Highway 47, Goodwood, Ontario,
    LOC 1A0 Canada
Phone: 905-640-6677
Website: www.richters.com
A large selection of herb seed, plants, dried
    herbs, and herb-related products.

SC Foundation Seed Association
1162 Cherry Rd., Box 349952, Clemson,
    SC 29634-9952
Phone: 864-656-2520
Fax: 864-656-1320
E-mail: seedw@clemson.edu
Website: www.clemson.edu/seed
Varieties developed for South Carolina
    (great for the rest of the South, too) and
    heirlooms.

Seeds for the South
410 Whaley Pond Road, Graniteville, SC
    29829
Fax: 803-232-1119
E-mail: orders@vegetableseedwarehouse.com
Website: www.seedsforthesouth.com/
Lots of southern-adapted herb and vegetable
    seeds—including heirlooms.

Seeds of Change
PO Box 15700, Santa Fe, NM 87506-
    5700
Phone: 888-762-7333
E-mail: gardener@seedsofchange.com
Website: www.seedsofchange.com
Source for organic seeds—flowers, herbs,
    and vegetables. Lots of gardening
    accessories and books.

Seed Savers Exchange
3094 North Winn Road, Decorah, IA
    52101
Phone: 563-382-5990
Fax: 563-382-5872

Website: www.seedsavers.org
Catalog specializes in heirloom varieties.

Southern Exposure Seed Exchange
PO Box 460, Mineral, VA 23117
Phone: 540-894-9480
Fax 540-894-9481
Catalog: $2.00. Lots of unusual and
    heirloom varieties.

Sproutpeople
170 Mendell St., San Francisco, CA
    94124
Phone: 877-777-6887
Website: www.sproutpeople.com
Want to do your own sprouts? This is the
    place for seeds, equipment, and books.

Stokes Seeds, Inc.
Box 548, Buffalo, NY 14240-0548
Phone: 800-263-7233; customer service,
    716-695-6980
Fax: 888-834-3334
E-mail: stokes@stokesseeds.com
Website: www.stokesseeds.com/cgi-bin/
    StokesSeeds.storefront
Free catalog. Beautiful color catalog and
    many of the varieties are great in
    southern gardens.

Territorial Seed Company
PO Box 158, Cottage Grove, OR 97424-
    0061
Phone: 800-626-0866
Fax: 888-657-3131
Website: www.territorialseed.com
Interesting seeds, plants, and supplies
    including mushroom kits.

Thompson & Morgan, Inc.
PO Box 1308, Jackson, NJ 08527-0308
Phone: 800-274-7333
Fax: 888-466-4769
Website: www.thompson-morgan.com
Free catalog. This is an English company
    with a U.S. distributor, so the seed is
    rather expensive.

Tomato Growers Supply Company
PO Box 2237, Ft. Myers, FL 33902

Phone: 888-478-7333; customer service,
    941-768-1119
Fax: 888-768-3476
Website: www.tomatogrowers.com
Lots of tomato varieties and an extensive list
    of sweet and hot peppers.

Totally Tomatoes
PO Box 1626, Augusta, GA 30903-1626
Phone: 803-663-0016
Fax: 888-477-7333
Website: www.totallytomato.com
Another specialty catalog with lots of
    tomatoes and peppers.

Veseys Seeds Ltd.
PO Box 9000, Calais, ME 04619-6102
Phone: 800-363-7333
Fax: 800-686-0329
Website: www.veseys.com
Lots of unusual and hard-to-find varieties.

Willhite Seed Co.
PO Box 23, Poolville, TX 76487
Phone: 817-599-8656; orders only, 800-
    828-1840
Fax: 817-599-5843
Website: www.willhiteseed.com
Free catalog. This Texas seed company used
    to be mostly a melon seed supplier. Now
    it has a wide range of vegetable varieties
    adapted to the South, plus wildflowers
    and even some exotic vegetable varieties
    from France and India. Still a great
    source for melon seeds.

WoodPrairie Farm
49 Kinney Road, Bridgewater, ME 04735
Phone: 800-829-9765
Website: www.woodprairie.com
A producer of organically grown potatoes,
    many varieties—including hard to find
    and heirloom—for planting or eating.

about the authors

William D. Adams is the Texas regional director of the Garden Writers Association and county extension agent emeritus in horticulture at Texas A&M. He is the coauthor of *The Lone Star Gardener's Book of Lists*. He lives in Burton, Texas.

Thomas R. LeRoy is coauthor (with Bill Adams) of *Commonsense Vegetable Gardening for the South*. He lives in Conroe, Texas.